POETRY FROM BABYLONIA AND ASSYRIA

Assurbanipal hunting onagers.
Relief from the North Palace of Assurbanipal at Nineveh.

Your thwarts in pieces
Your mooring rope cut

Poetry from Babylonia and Assyria

Erica Reiner

Published by
Horace H. Rackham School
of Graduate Studies
at the University of Michigan

© 1985 by the University of Michigan
ISBN 0-936534-04-4

Michigan Studies in the Humanities, 5
Published by
Horace H. Rackham School of Graduate Studies
at the University of Michigan

Board of Editors

Richard Bailey (English), Judith Becker (Music), Arthur Burks (Philosophy), Oscar Büdel (Italian), Vern Carroll (Anthropology), Herbert Eagle (Film), Emery George (German), Floyd Gray (French), D. Kirkpatrick (History of Art), Ladislav Matejka (Slavic), Walter Mignolo (Spanish), Eric Rabkin (American Studies), G. Rosenwald (Psychology), Ingo Seidler (German), Gernot Windfuhr (Near Eastern Studies).

Irwin R. Titunik, *Associate Editor*
Ladislav Matejka, *Managing Editor*

Cover. K. 890 (cuneiform tablet inscribed with the Assyrian Elegy, from the library of Assurbanipal at Nineveh). Reproduced by courtesy of the Trustees of the British Museum.

Pp. ii-iii. Assurbanipal hunting onagers. Relief from the North Palace of Assurbanipal at Nineveh. Reproduced by courtesy of the Trustees of the British Museum.

P. 28. Assurbanipal and his queen relaxing in the royal park. Relief from the North Palace of Assurbanipal at Nineveh. Reproduced by courtesy of the Trustees of the British Museum.

P. 60. Two lion-griffins attacking bull between them. Middle Assyrian cylinder seal (14th cent. B.C.) in the Pierpont Morgan Library Collection, New York.

CONTENTS

Introduction ix

I. Two Kings
   1. Nabonidus and the Concern with the Past   1
   2. Assurbanipal and the Legitimation by the Present   17

II. Two Poems about the Nether World
   1. The Descent of Ištar: From Myth to Narrative   29
   2. Nergal and Ereškigal: Epic into Romance   48

III. The News of Victory   61

IV. A Hymn to the Sun   68

V. Lyric Poetry
   1. An Assyrian Elegy   85
   2. Poem about the Heart-Grass   94

VI. "This Year and into the Next . . .": The Second Tablet of *Ludlul bēl nēmeqi*—Intricate Texture of a Learned Poem   101

Herrlich ist der Orient
Übers Mittelmeer gedrungen
Nur wer Hafis liebt und kennt
Weiss was Calderon gesungen.

      West-östlicher Divan

INTRODUCTION

Some of the earliest records of civilization, the texts written down in ancient Mesopotamia in the Assyro-Babylonian language, are poems. But their number is dwarfed by the vast amounts of archival material—ledgers and other administrative texts, legal documents, and other records of daily life—that begin around 2400 B.C. and continue to proliferate on tens of thousands of clay tablets well into the Hellenistic age. This documentation is increasingly being used to reconstruct not only social and economic history but intellectual history as well.

Much less prominent in the reconstruction of Mesopotamian cultural and intellectual history have been its poetic works. This cannot be due to lack of interest in or acquaintance with them; the major literary works of the Babylonians have long been known; many have been translated into modern European languages; and a person with some literary culture is familiar with at least the Epic of Gilgamesh and often with other Babylonian poetry. For a long time now these works have served as comparative material to Old Testament scholars and, more recently, to students of comparative religion.

Babylonian literature has fared less well in being appreciated for its intrinsic merit. It has received less attention from literary historians, either as a representative of an ancient literature or as a stage in the development of Western literature. Thus, paradoxically, poetic works have contributed little to our awareness of the intellectual and artistic aspirations of this more than four-thousand-year-old civilization.

The obvious fact that the literature of an ancient and alien culture is difficult to apprehend by a taste sharpened on the classics and on European literature cannot by itself explain the neglect of the role of Mesopotamian literary creations in the history of literature. In fact, it seems to me, it is their very content that has precluded their assimilation into literary history. The stories they tell are in themselves so strange and fascinating that they have been claimed as relevant to fields extraneous to literature: to the history of religions, the study of myths, or even the so-called "primitive" or "pre-logical" mentality. Engrossing as these stories may be, their motifs and their *fabula* alone can tell us little about the literary aspirations of Babylonian poets or the preferences of their public.

The legitimate concerns of historians of religion need not overshadow the literary appreciation of Babylonian poetic works. This task, which ideally a trained literary historian should perform, today still needs the care of the philologist who reads these works in the original. Apart from the philologist's basic task of establishing the meanings of rare and little-known words—a task often made more difficult by the nature of the cuneiform writing system wherein a syllabic sign, even if undamaged and completely legible, is susceptible of several readings—and of resolving the grammatical ambiguities inherent in the morphology or syntax of Akkadian, it is his familiarity with a large body of texts that allows him to perceive both the unusual and the atypical in diction and the echoes and allusions among a varied spectrum of poetical works.

In recent years, some Near Eastern scholars have begun to look at their sources as expressions of literary creativity. Several of their studies have been inspired by the textual analysis of Roman Jakobson, by the motif analysis of V. Propp, or by other contemporary structuralists. They have treated individual texts (though mostly Sumerian ones); classified a particular genre; or made claims about the methodology for an entire vast corpus.[1] All of these studies have appeared in publications that address the cuneiformist. To my knowledge, none have addressed the reader outside this specialized field, whether the literary historian or the so-called "educated layman." Their merit has been that of introducing to their field concepts not generally current among philologists and of explicating and applying techniques proven on texts from the world's other literatures; still, they speak to an audience familiar with the basic assumptions underlying their textual analysis—the religious setting, the poetic conventions, and the linguistic and philological ambiguities of a Sumerian or Akkadian text.

To present these texts to an outsider, especially to a literary historian long familiar with the various schools of literary criticism, the emphasis must lie precisely on those features that are obvious to the Near Eastern scholar. For example, while translations should not make the text unintelligible by adhering to Assyriological conventions that sound quaint to all but the expert, a translator who wishes to render an ancient text in a modern, poetic form is, I believe, also duty bound to explain at some point of his presentation how the ancient poet achieved his effects with the means at his disposal. This may necessitate quoting certain lines in a literal translation, so as to illustrate the formal devices (parallelism, repetition, etc.) characteristic of this literature, and even in the original Akkadian (in the conventional transcription system) to indicate the poem's sound pattern. Since the Babylonians did not leave us an *Ars poetica*, only by such attention to detail can poetic conventions, literary preferences, or changes in taste be inferred.

The Assyriologist knows that it is too early to attempt to write a history of Babylonian literature. In fact, he has so often said it—invoking the force of tradition responsible for preserving and perpetuating texts over hundreds, and possibly thousands, of years and thus allowing no real development—that he has been generally believed. Yet Babylonian literature is not as static and immutable as might be suggested by finds of nearly identical copies of some composition written down hundreds of years apart—a frequent phenomenon that is the despair of the historian but a boon to the philologist who can use similar exemplars to reconstruct a fragmentary text. In what measure identical exemplars reflect the immutability of tradition and, conversely, in what measure changes observed between an earlier and a later exemplar are indicators of a change in taste and interest are important questions for the interpretation of Babylonian literary history that only much painstaking philological work will elucidate.

Nevertheless, it is possible to use some selected texts as case studies to point up facts and trends that a survey or some other generalized approach necessarily has to gloss over. My selections in this book intend to illustrate some of the ways in which this literature can be approached to yield increased insight and appreciation.

If one is to show why and how a poetic text achieved the status it had among the Babylonians—a status that is evident by its inclusion in a royal or temple library or in the collection of a scholar, by references to it in catalogues or instructions for oral performance, and not least by direct quotes from it in other literary works—the text needs a detailed analysis and commentary, an approach nowadays often called close reading but which used to be termed, more poetically, a loving immersion. This approach pays attention not only to the structure of the whole and its intertextual relationships but also to the formal—linguistic or metric—devices that distinguish poetry from ordinary prose.

Since many of the formal devices that are obvious in or can be elicited from the original text are easily lost in a translated version, my choices were guided by the ease of access to the formal as well as the structural properties of the text. My translations are often more literal than necessary; their literalness, while sacrificing poetic effect, may help the reader develop his own appreciation for the linguistic impact of these poems.

It is also proper to state what texts I have not included in this collection. Absent is the most discussed, the longest and best known, and probably the greatest masterpiece of Babylonian literature, the Gilgamesh Epic. Absent also is the much more recently completely recovered poem about the Creation of Man, also called Atrahasis from the name of its human hero, the survivor of the Flood, who also appears, under a different name, in the famous story of the Flood in the Gilgamesh Epic. My reasons for excluding these and other epics were not only their relative familiarity or even their length but also the fact that the narration of their plots, especially in a streamlined form, would detract attention from the literary analysis that is my primary aim in this book. As well known as these stories are, from having been anthologized and used by historians of religion and cultural anthropologists, they represent a small fraction of the extant literature of the Babylonians. Indeed, compared to the number of varied and as yet unexhausted Sumerian narrative poems of an earlier age about the rivalries and amorous adventures of the gods, the number of Babylonian poems concerned with the gods and mythological topics seems to have noticeably diminished. Any survey of Babylonian literature would be disproportionately weighted by the space needed to treat such epics or legends, which more properly belong in a study of Babylonian religion.[2]

Still, no picture of Babylonian literature is complete without some mythological poems. I have included two (in Chapter II) and briefly treated motifs of two others (in Chapter III). If my choice fell, among mythological topics, on the two poems set in the nether world, it is because they show something beyond the mythopoeic imagination that has captivated Western scholars. In fact, the first, the Descent of Ishtar, is witness to the transformation of the Sumerian myth about the Descent of Inanna (Ishtar's Sumerian counterpart), most recently interpreted by G. S. Kirk and T. Jacobsen, into an interesting story, which, notwithstanding its divine and demonic actors, pays hardly any attention to the themes of fertility cycles on earth that are at the center of the Sumerian myth. The second poem, about Nergal and Ereshkigal, is one of the few literary works for which two versions, an older and a more recent one, can be compared to illustrate how a story about the gods, originally probably an etiological myth, became, through the addition of episodes of complex peripeties, a romance.

Lyric and philosophical poetry, deeply religious but bound by traditional themes and expressions of the relation between gods and man, has often been adduced as foil for the Psalms, in which many echoes of the Babylonian poems' diction can be discerned. In dealing with such examples of Babylonian poetry (Chapters IV and VI) I have focused instead on the architectonic structure of the Hymn to the Sun God and of one canto of the so-called Babylonian Job. Of the many features that articulate the structure of these two long poems, the more formal patterns of syntax, vocabulary, and even grammar could best be shown by the sort of interpretive technique that was introduced by Roman Jakobson, a technique that, whatever valid objections contemporary literary criticism has raised against it, can still effectively point up the grammatical interrelations or sound-patterning of a poem. This technique is only now reaching the specialists of ancient Near Eastern literatures, and a demonstration and test of its applicability was one of my aims in so treating not only the religious or philosophical poems of Chapters IV and VI but especially the shorter poems of Chapter V.

Yet it is not only lyric or narrative poetry that gives the measure of Babylonian literature. There is a vast corpus of prose literature, of a historiographic nature: the accounts of Assyrian and Babylonian kings of their military achievements in expanding their empires as representatives of the national god, and of their equally essential care of the gods and their shrines. These historical, annalistic, and at times autobiographical narratives that express the prevailing royal ideology cunningly manipulate events for the edification of contemporary audiences as well as for posterity. To illustrate the tenor of these royal statements I have chosen one inscription each from Babylonia and Assyria. By placing them in the first chapter, I hope to situate Babylonian literature in relation to particular historical moments across which arch the more timeless religious and mythological poems of the later chapters. I also mean to stress thereby that this literature is culture-bound and not to be sought in the haze of mythological times and moreover that its sophistication is not dependent on the well-worn poetic devices of repetition and parallelism alone. Hitherto, historical texts received attention mostly as illustrating royal ideologies and propaganda, in an intellectual context, or in a historical context as contributing to the emergence of the Assyrian empire; my emphasis here is on the formal sophistication that enabled the poets in the kings' service to insinuate as well as proclaim the royal ideology in a masterful way. It is thus a first step in the direction indicated by A. L. Oppenheim who believed that "the easy accessibility of these texts, first to those scholars who were merely interested in their language and then to those who were concentrating on their historical data, has for some time prevented us from realizing that they are indeed literary creations and that they should be studied as such."[3]

NOTES

1. P. Michalowski, "Carminative Magic: Towards an Understanding of Sumerian Poetics," *Zeitschrift für Assyriologie* 71 (1981) pp. 1-18; B. Alster, *Dumuzi's Dream. Aspects of Oral Poetry in a Sumerian Myth.* (= Mesopotamia, vol. 1). Copenhagen: Akademisk Forlag 1972; K. Hecker, *Untersuchungen zur akkadischen Epik.* Alter Orient und Altes Testament Sonderreihe, vol. 8. Neukirchen-Vluyn: Neukirchener Verlag 1974; W. R. Mayer, *Untersuchungen zur Formensprache der babylonischen "Gebetsbeschwörungen."* (= Studia Pohl: Series Maior 5). Rome: Biblical Institute Press 1976; C. Wilcke, "Formale Gesichtspunkte in der sumerischen Literatur," Sumerological Studies in Honor of Thorkild Jacobsen (= *Assyriological Studies* 20). Chicago: University of Chicago Press (1976) pp. 205-260. See also J. Sasson, *Ruth: A New Translation with a Philological Commentary and a Formalist-Folklorist Interpretation.* Baltimore: Johns Hopkins University Press 1979.

2. As they were treated, for example, by René Labat, "Les grands textes de la pensée babylonienne," in *Les religions du Proche-Orient asiatique*, part 1. Paris: Fayard-Denoël (1970) pp. 15-349.

3. A. L. Oppenheim, "Neo-Assyrian and Neo-Babylonian Empires," in *Propaganda and Communication in World History*. Vol. 1, *The Symbolic Instrument in Early Times*, eds., Harold D. Lasswell, Daniel Lerner, and Hans Speier. Honolulu: The University Press of Hawaii 1979, p. 117.

It was my good fortune to be involved for many years in the Assyrian Dictionary Project of the University of Chicago, where I learned, under the guidance of Benno Landsberger and Leo Oppenheim, how important it is both to perceive and account for every detail of a text and to integrate it into the culture that it documents. I can acknowledge my debt to them only in this most inadequate way, dedicating this book to their memory.

My friends and colleagues associated with the project in various ways gave me not only encouragement but also constructive criticism on the book or selected chapters, without insisting that I follow their specific suggestions. I greatly profited from illuminating discussions on Babylonian literature and many related matters with J. A. Brinkman, M. Civil, D. O. Edzard, Hans Hirsch, Hermann Hunger, Simo Parpola, Johannes Renger, and M. W. Stolper, which it is my pleasure to acknowledge here. For turning my prose into readable English, I am indebted to the taste and style of Julie Robinson.

Many other friends were equally generous in giving me the benefit of their experiences with and insights into the world's less known literatures, in particular Peter Dembowski and Arnaldo Momigliano. The initial impetus for my work came from Svetozàr Petrović, Professor of Comparative Literature at the University of Belgrade, to whose continuous interest and unfailing encouragement it is due, without any doubt, that this book reached its present form.

Chapter I

TWO KINGS

1. NABONIDUS AND THE CONCERN WITH THE PAST

After the Assyrian empire had fallen to the Medes (Nineveh, the capital, fell in 612 B.C.), Babylonia alone continued to consider itself the depositary of Mesopotamian culture. The sixth-century kings of the Neo-Babylonian or Chaldean dynasty, a ruling house itself a newcomer to the Babylonian scene, acted as heirs of their predecessors of one thousand years earlier and beyond. Especially Nebuchadnezzar and Nabonidus modeled their writings on those of the famed Akkad dynasty of the late third millennium and of the glorious age of Hammurapi and his successors in the early second. They wrote not annals of wars, as the Assyrian kings had done, but elaborate votive inscriptions. They wrote in what we presume was the contemporary Babylonian literary idiom in which scholarly literature and belles-lettres were also written, as opposed to the Neo-Babylonian dialect used in letters and legal texts. But the writings of these kings contain many features that presuppose a deliberate study of ancient royal inscriptions. That such inscriptions had survived to their time would be unmistakable from the graphic patterns, spellings, and phrases imitating—sometimes incorrectly—these ancient texts even if it were not often described how the Neo-Babylonian kings searched for and found in the ruins of some building the original foundation inscription of an early predecessor.[1]

The cultivation of models from the past went hand in hand with a renewed interest in Sumerian, the language that Akkadian had supplanted and which survived only in certain liturgical texts and, after a fashion, in the scholarly literature. Scholars continued to compile Sumerian words and phrases, providing them with Akkadian translations, and scholarly texts had always made abundant use of Sumerian word signs within an Akkadian context, mainly as a technical vocabulary that also fulfilled the role of shorthand since an inflected Akkadian word that may routinely require three to four cuneiform signs, and often more, can be written with a single Sumerogram with, occasionally, not more than one additional sign as a phonetic complement when the Sumerogram's referent must be made explicit. The use of such Sumerograms in nontechnical texts, however, is much more rare and restricted. Yet the Chaldean dynasty kings all of a sudden began to pepper their inscriptions with elaborate, often quite unusual, Sumerian phrases. They sought to imitate, this practice shows, ancient inscriptions written not only in Akkadian but also in Sumerian, thus exhibiting their learnedness in the use of language as well as in the use of archaic sign forms and sign values. Along with the language, these kings revived ancient customs and ancient gods, or lent ancient names to the gods of the day.

The reasons behind this search for things past must have been complex and, though far from transparent, no doubt stemmed from political considerations as much as from the kings' personal interests and preferences; their well-known antiquarianism must have served purposes other than the recovery of ancient inscriptions and objects in their enviably successful excavations. The interplay of the ancient and modern makes this period of less than one hundred years in the history of Babylonia, before it came to share in the fortunes of the Persian empire in which it was englobed if not integrated, a fascinating chapter of intellectual history that is yet to be explored. Still, even one of the surviving texts may serve as the starting point to such a study; such a text will be my sole concern here.

(I) 1.   When Nannar requested a high priestess
the Son of the Prince showed his sign to the inhabited world;
the Bright-Light manifested his reliable decision.
To Nabonidus, king of Babylon, provider for Esagil and Ezida,
5.   the reverent shepherd, who shows concern for the sanctuaries of the great gods
Nannar, the lord of the crown, who bears the signal for all peoples,
revealed his sign concerning his request for a high priestess.
On the thirteenth of Ulūlu, the month of the work of goddesses,
the Fruit became eclipsed and set while eclipsed.
10.   "Sin requests a high priestess"—such was his sign and decision.
As for me, Nabonidus, the shepherd who reveres his divine majesty, I reverently heeded his reliable order,
so that I became concerned about this request for a high priestess.
I sought out the sanctuaries of Šamaš and Adad, the patrons of extispicy,
15.   and Šamaš and Adad, as usual, answered me a reliable yes,
wrote a favorable omen in my extispicy,
the omen pertaining to the request for priestesses, the request of the gods to man.
I repeated the extispicy for confirmation and they answered me with an even more favorable omen.

I made an extispicy inquiring about a daughter born to one of my relatives, but they answered me no.
20. A third time I made an extispicy inquiring about my own daughter and they answered me with a favorable omen.
I heeded the word of Sin, the supreme lord, the god my creator,
and the verdict of Šamaš and Adad, the patrons of extispicy;
I installed my own daughter as high priestess
25. and gave her the name En-nigaldi-Nanna.
Because for a very long time the office of high priestess had been forgotten
and her characteristic features were nowhere indicated, I bethought myself day after day.
The appointed time having arrived, the doors were opened for me;
Indeed I set eyes on an ancient stele of Nebuchadnezzar,
30. son of Ninurta-nadin-šumi, an early king of the past,
on which was depicted the image of the high priestess;
moreover, they had listed and deposited in the Egipar
her appurtenances, her clothing, and her jewelry.
I carefully looked into the old clay and wooden tablets
35. and did exactly as in the olden days.
A stele, her appurtenances, and her household equipment
I fashioned anew, respectively inscribed on it,
and deposited it before my lord and lady Sin and Ningal.

(II) At that time Egipar, the holy precinct, wherein the rites of the high priestess used to be carried out,
40. was an abandoned place, and had become a heap of ruins,
palm trees and orchard fruit were growing in its midst.
I cut down the trees, removed the rubble of its ruins,
I set eyes on the temple and its foundation terrace became visible.
Inside it I set eyes on inscriptions of old earlier kings,
45. I also set eyes on an old inscription of En-ane-du, high priestess of Ur,
daughter of Kudur-Mabuk, sister of Rim-Sin, king of Ur,
who renovated Egipar and restored it,
and surrounded with a wall the resting place of the old high priestesses adjoining Egipar,
so that I made Egipar (too) anew as in the olden days,
50. I built its daises and plans anew as in the olden days,
I made anew the house of my daughter En-nigaldi-Nanna, high priestess of Sin, adjoining Egipar.

		I consecrated my daughter and dedicated her to my lord and lady Sin and Ningal.

            I consecrated my daughter and dedicated her to my lord and
                lady Sin and Ningal.
            Through the art of the exorcist I purified her and introduced
                her into Egipar.
            I made the regular offerings of Egipar plentiful,
55.   I granted it abundant fields, orchards, slaves, cattle, and sheep.
            The resting place of the ancient priestesses
            I surrounded with a wall as in the olden days,
            I made that house into a secure place.

(III)   At that time for my lord and lady Sin and Ningal
      60.   I made their regular offerings more plentiful than before,
            I made all kinds of things abundant in Ekišnugal.
            For every day I established for my lord and lady Sin and
                Ningal three sheep instead of the one sheep, the old regular
                offering;
            I made abundant in Ekišnugal all kinds of goods and treasures.
            In order to perform with the proper holiness the sacrifices, so
                that no error may occur,
      65.   the consecrated personnel of Ekišnugal and of the temples:
            the high priest, the purification priest, the *zabardabbu,* the
                diviner, the cook,
            the miller, the master builder, the builder, the courtyard
                sweeper, the chief doorkeeper,
            the *court attendant,* the priest who performs rites of homage,
            the singers who gladden the gods' hearts,
      70.   the collegium of priests here enumerated,
            I released from their feudal obligations, exempted them, freed
                them,
            and gave them without encumbrance to my lord and lady Sin
                and Ningal.

(IV)   O Sin, holy god, lord of the crown, light of mankind,
            supreme god whose command is reliable
      75.   may he rejoice at my actions, love my kingship,
            grant me long life, the satisfaction of old age,
            raise no rival to me so that I have none to vie with me.
            With each month may signs of good portent manifest themselves for me,
            may the crown of my kingship be firm on my head forever.
      80.   Make my throne firm for all days to come.
            With each month, when you renew yourself
            let me set eyes regularly on your good signal.

> May Ningal, the supreme lady, always speak good for me before you.
> May En-nigaldi-Nanna, my own beloved daughter,
> 85. live happily in your presence and may her command be reliable,
> 86a. may her actions please you,
> 86b. may she commit no error.

The text is inscribed on a baked clay cylinder found at Ur. It deals with the dedication of Nabonidus' daughter as high priestess of the Moon god, an event to which Nabonidus alludes in other inscriptions[2] but which here is the central topic.

The custom of a person of royal lineage serving as priestess of the Moon god in the city of Ur ("Ur of the Chaldees") is well documented from the time of Sargon of Akkad (2334-2279 B.C.) to the time of Hammurapi (1792-1750). This priestess was chosen by an oracle imparted by the gods through extispicy—divination from the entrails of a sheep—, served the Moon god under his Sumerian name Nanna, and herself bore a Sumerian name even if she was an Akkadian princess.

When the center of administration of Babylonia, and by extension its religious center, was relocated to Babylon during the Hammurapi dynasty, this custom fell into disuse. Babylonian kings paid their special devotion to Marduk and his son Nabû. Only Nabonidus, breaking with this Babylon-centered cult of his immediate predecessors, directed his personal devotion to the Moon god—not the least of his eccentricities that the anti-Nabonidus faction exploited.

Nabonidus' account of the dedication of his daughter to the Moon god attests to his desire to present his actions, eccentric as they may have seemed to many, as part of the historical continuum, and thereby to integrate his reign into the glorious Babylonian past. It is a carefully composed document, on the surface conforming to the style and structure of pious royal inscriptions which record votive offerings for which the king expects the gods' blessing. Such inscriptions speak of rebuilding decayed temples and of lavishly furnishing them as appropriate residences for the god; the rebuilding of temples maintains a link with the past, but a past which is within memory and still visible, albeit deteriorated. In this inscription Nabonidus builds on a long-forgotten foundation; he has to create a bridge across centuries, bring about a revival and not simply a renewal.

Not only does Nabonidus revive the cult of the Moon god, prompted, no doubt, by his religious feeling, as he has been doing in Babylonia as well as in his favorite and perhaps ancestral city of Harran,[3] but he also effectively institutionalizes his personal devotion by reviving this cult in the city of Ur, the god's ancient seat in Babylonia. Ur, famed as capital of the Ur III empire (2112-2004 B.C.) and still propserous and important during the reigns of the dynasties of Isin and of Larsa over the next 250 years, never rose to its former influential position after its destruction around 1740 B.C. by the Babylonian king Samsuiluna.[4] What better way for Nabonidus to assure the god of his devotion and at the same time to establish a continuity over more than a millennium than to reinstitute the ancient practice of dedicating a royal princess as high priestess at the Moon god's temple in Ur?

If the revival of a custom that had lapsed for about 1200 years is emphasized, so is, subtly, its continuity. Between the eighteenth century and his own time Nabonidus creates a historical link by way of a famous twelfth-century king of Babylonia, Nebuchadnezzar I (1124-1103) (the namesake of Nabonidus' predecessor Nebuchadnezzar II whose throne he had usurped)—a link unsupported by independent evidence[5] and probably fictitious, created solely for this purpose.

The form given to this novel topic is that of the standard Neo-Babylonian votive inscriptions. They begin with a long and elaborate clause introduced by *īnu* 'when' and end with an invocation to the god asking his blessing on the king's handiwork and his reign. The central part, introduced by the adverb *inūšu* 'then,' narrates how the king carried out his pious project.

The inscription recording Nabonidus' dedication of his daughter also begins with *īnu* 'when'; it ends with a prayer introduced by the name of the god to whom the dedication is made. But the central part consists of two sections, each introduced by the counterpart of the 'when' conjunction, the adverb *inūšu* 'then,' 'at that time.' Thus its 86 lines fall into four parts, the first taking up 38 lines,[6] the second 20, the third 14, and the fourth and last also 14. It is immediately apparent that the first part is excessively long compared to the other three, which are roughly in balance—almost twice as long as the second, and almost three times as long as the last two.

The literary form of the division into a 'when' and a 'then' clause goes back to Sumerian prototypes; the expansion of the first, 'when,' section so as to enumerate the king's previous achievements is an innovation of the scribes who composed the Neo-Babylonian royal inscriptions.[7] But while Nebuchadnezzar, the first king to use this pattern in Akkadian, includes in the greatly expanded 'when' clause a description of his past activities, in this inscription Nabonidus in the 'when' clause dwells only on the events leading up to the installation of his daughter as high priestess.

These first 38 lines fall into three sections: the divine sign ordering the appointment of a high priestess (1-10); the verification of the exact wish of the god (11-25); and the providential find that enables Nabonidus to carry out this wish in accordance with the ancient rites (26-38).

The first departure from the customary pattern comes in the very first section. There is no introduction naming the king and his titles, and the *īnu* 'when' clause, instead of extending over several lines, consists of the single line, "When Nannar requested a high priestess." This is followed directly—in four pairs of lines—by an amplification of how the god communicated his request, an amplification in the form of a triple assertion of his having manifested a sign, stated twice in the first pair, and once again in the third. The first pair states, in two parallel phrases, that the moon god gave a sign:

> The Son of the Prince showed his sign to the inhabited world;
> the Bright-Light manifested his reliable decision.

Only in the second pair is the king introduced, not yet as the speaker nor as the actor, but rather in an oblique way as the person to whom this sign was revealed, as the third pair of lines finally states:

> To Nabonidus, king of Babylon, provider for Esagil and Ezida,
> the reverent shepherd, who shows concern for the sanctuaries of the great gods,
> Nannar, the lord of the crown, who bears the signal for all peoples,
> revealed his sign concerning his request for a high priestess.

The last pair of lines describes the sign itself: a lunar eclipse. Another single line, the final line of this section, rather dramatically sums up the situation: the sign was interpreted to the effect that the Moon god requested a high priestess. The sign's interpretation—the first half of this line—"Sin requests a high priestess" is none other than a repetition of the first line except for the inverted word order and the use of the Semitic name Sin for the Moon god rather than his Sumerian name Nanna(r).

This first mention of the Akkadian name Sin serves to provide the link between the event—the lunar eclipse—and the Babylonian compendium of celestial omens in which the interpretation of the eclipse was sought and found, since all lunar omens designate the Moon by the name of Sin. Before this tenth line the Moon god, whom Nabonidus usually addresses with this name Sin, is designated by a variety of names and epithets: Nannar (line 1), *mār rubê* 'Son of the Prince' (line 2), *Namra-ṣēt* 'Bright-Light' (line 3), again Nannar (line 6), and *Inbu* 'Fruit' (line 9). These terms not only provide stylistic variation but also set the stage and, as they are ancient, Sumerian or Sumerianizing names, they prepare for the interpretation of the Moon god's sign as calling for a revival of an ancient custom. The use of these names also adroitly avoids an association of the events with the new-fangled Western cult of Sin that Nabonidus had introduced.

In fact, the only lines in this introductory section that tie it to other Neo-Babylonian votive inscriptions are the two which contain the king's name and epithets. Foremost among these is the title "king of Babylon, provider for Esagil and Ezida," that is, for the temples of the god Marduk and his son Nabû, Esagil being the main sanctuary of Marduk, city god of Babylon and by this time supreme god of Babylonia. By the choice of this title Nabonidus emphasizes that he places himself in the contemporaneous, accepted framework of Babylonian ideology, not only in the historical continuum of the Moon god's cult.

The interpretation of the lunar eclipse as the god's request for a high priestess is given in line 10 without naming the source of this interpretation. The source, as has long been recognized, is a chapter of *Enūma Anu Enlil*, the Babylonian compendium of celestial omens; the omen also appears in a compilation modern scholars call "The Babylonian Calendar," which contains excerpts from celestial omens arranged according to the twelve months of the year.[8]

These were the sources the Babylonian scholars turned to for ascertaining the portent of celestial signs, and where they have found the entry "If Sin is eclipsed in the month of Ulūlu in the last watch of the night"—i.e., in the sixth month at dawn—"Sin requests a high priestess," just as we, having access to these very sources, have found it too.

Yet Nabonidus mentions nothing of this process, nor does he quote the complete omen as it appears in the compendium.[9] Rather, only the apodosis is quoted verbatim: "Sin requests a high priestess." The protasis, the eclipse itself, is paraphrased in poetic language. This is achieved by calling the Moon not Sin, the name used in the celestial omen texts, but by its epithet "Fruit," an epithet that also appears in the title of the Babylonian royal hemerologies (calendars listing favorable and unfavorable days and prescribing or forbidding certain activities on each), *Inbu bēl arhi* 'The Fruit, the lord of the month,' to designate the Moon, a waxing—growing—fruit.[10] Moreover, instead of simply giving the date of the eclipse—the 13th of the month of Ulūlu—with the name of the month written, as customary, with a Sumerogram, the text adds a translation of the month name. The translation is not the expected corresponding Akkadian month name *Ulūlu* undoubtedly intended by the Sumerogram ITI.KIN.^{d}INANNA but a literal translation of its constituent elements ITI = *arhu*, KIN = *šipru*, ^{d}INANNA = *ištar*; the resulting Akkadian phrase *arah šipir ištarāti* 'the month of the work of the goddesses' is an occasionally-used learned, but unfortunately opaque, designation for this, the sixth month of the year. Our only clue to its meaning comes from "Astrolabe B," a compilation which, in addition to astronomical material, also gives Sumero-Akkadian etymological explanations for the names of the months; in this text "the month of the work of the goddesses" is said to be the time when "the goddesses purify themselves in the river, cleanse themselves every year." Scribes of earlier kings, those of Sargon and the Sargonids in eighth and seventh century Assyria, similarly exhibited their learning by word-for-word translations of the commonly used Sumerograms for month names into such descriptive phrases, and thus introduced into their descriptions of events an appoggiatura which seems to have remained a favored literary conceit.

It is not the form alone that sets this lunar omen apart from a mere quotation from the compendium. What gives the interpretation of the omen its special character and situates it in a context much earlier than the first millennium setting is the fact that the portent given by the lunar eclipse did not provide the required certainty. It had to be checked by that most ancient of Mesopotamian divinatory methods, the one considered the most reliable, namely, extispicy.

In the first millennium, when portents derived from celestial phenomena acquired increasing importance over other forms of divination, celestial omens were interpreted on their own merit, as numerous reports from scholars versed in this form of divination attest. In the second millennium, however, the portent of an eclipse—and the truth of oracular utterances—had to be checked by means of extispicy.[11] The lunar eclipse under Nabonidus was submitted to the same verification. This consultation is the subject of the next section of the inscription, lines 11-25.

It is a consultation in three stages: an extispicy is made first to confirm the portent of the eclipse through the portent given by the configuration of the exta (usually the liver); the result of this extispicy is double-checked through a repetition of the procedure, a repetition often routinely carried out, as other reports on extispicies inform us. The first extispicy confirmed the god's wish for a high priestess; of its repetition the king states only that it was even more favorable than the first. Nabonidus then seeks to specify the portent by means of another consultation—the second stage, although technically the third inspection of the exta—asking whether a certain princess of the royal family is to be the high priestess; the answer to this query is "no." In a third consultation he asks about the suitability of his own daughter, and now the answer given by the extispicy is favorable.

The report on the consultations is styled as an inquiry addressed to Šamaš and Adad, the patron gods of extispicy. The answer given by the gods, each time in the same terms, is expressed by the verb *ītappalu(in)ni* 'they answered me ("yes" or "no")'; this verb occurs at the end of lines 15, 18, 19, and 21. Only the first "yes" answer is followed by the elaboration that the gods inscribed a favorable sign in the liver, an image familiar from poetic texts but not part of the technical vocabulary of the haruspex—the diviner who examined the sheep's entrails. The query too is couched in the repeated simple terms: *têrtu ēpušma* 'I made an extispicy'; no mention is made of the expert who actually performed it, the diviner. Since the king's query and the gods' answer are expressed in simple phrases, only their cumulation and the gradation expressed by 'a second time' (line 18), 'a third time' (line 20) convey the sense of culmination which is achieved when the gods of extispicy finally approve the king's daughter as suitable to be installed as high priestess.

This detailed description not only gives a precise report on the method of checking the significance of a celestial omen through extispicy[12]—and incidentally also confirms what we know from other sources, that in this period the examination of the exta no longer sought portents applying to specific situations but requested merely a yes-or-no answer—but also artfully builds up to a climax through narrowing down the portent of the eclipse, from the god's wish for an unspecified high priestess to the inquiry about some princess of royal blood, until finally the king's daughter is designated by the extispicy as the high priestess desired by the Moon god.

The next four lines describe the king's acceptance of the god's wish in a simple and factual reporting style. The simplicity is manifested in the syntactic construction of three coordinate clauses, each with its predicate in final, that is, unmarked, position:

> I heeded the word of Sin, the supreme lord, the god my creator,
> and the verdict of Šamaš and Adad, the patrons of extispicy;
> I installed my own daughter as high priestess
> and gave her the name En-nigaldi-Nanna.[13]

This new, official name given to Nabonidus' daughter is a Sumerian name. It is similar in structure to the names of her predecessors in office, names all beginning with the word *en* 'high priestess.'[14] The name En-nigaldi-Nanna, meaning 'High Priestess requested by Nanna,' is here not just another poetic name; it not only alludes to the circumstances of her calling, but is in fact none other than a nominalization of the omen "Sin requests a high priestess" and of the first line, "Nannar requested a high priestess."

The third section of the introduction describes the miraculous event of the discovery of an ancient stela depicting the high priestess and describing the appurtenances of the office; without this information the proper installation of Nabonidus' daughter could not have taken place. The supernatural intervention is signaled by a shift to impersonal verbs in this single line 28, a contrast with the rest of the inscription which narrates the events in the first person, with only an occasional third-person form introduced when appropriate. In the preceding two lines the king still speaks himself, relating his own actions:

> Because for a very long time the office of high priestess had been forgotten
> and her characteristic features were nowhere indicated, I bethought myself day after day *(ūmišam uštaddan)*.

The impersonal line is now introduced:

> *adannu ikšudamma uptattâni bābāni* 'The appointed time having arrived, the doors were opened for me.'

The appointed time *(adannu)* usually designates a preordained or a precalculated point in time; it is surely an intentional echo-word following on the line-closing *uštaddan* of the preceding line. And as the text reverts to first-person narrative, the first such verb, *appalisma* 'I set eyes on,' is now placed in line-initial, that is, marked, position.

The strange phrase "the doors were opened for me" seems to contain a metaphor, since no reference is made to the circumstances surrounding the discovery of the stela and of the tablets—both clay and wooden tablets—found with it.

With the account of the discovery of the stela[15] we have come to the end of the first part, the part that goes from the introductory *īnu* to the central *inūšu*. In the last four lines Nabonidus states that he executed what was to be done *kīma labīrimma* 'as of old' (line 35) and that he fashioned anew *(eššiš abni)* a stela which he inscribed and dedicated to Sin and his spouse Ningal. These two phrases, "as of old" and "I fashioned (made, etc.) anew" recur from here onward: the first in lines 49, 50, and 57, and the second in lines 49, 50, 51, and 57. The two motifs, the following of the old models and the restoration of old statues, stelas, buildings, cults, are the key concepts in Babylonian piety: the king, when rebuilding a temple, follows the ground plan of his predecessors, and he in turn enjoins his successors even in the remote future to do exactly as he himself has done. The old and the new are thus inextricably interwoven in Babylonian religious practice, and they are so conjoined in the two consecutive lines 49 and 50, as they end, not out of carelessness of diction, not inadvertently, but on purpose and emphatically: *kīma labīrimma eššiš ēpuš* (49), *kīma labīrimma eššiš abni* (50).[16]

Indeed, the most frequent term in this text, even more frequent than the apparent key word *entu* 'priestess' that occurs seven times, is the word *labīru* 'old,' 'ancient,' which appears eight times qualifying customs, cult objects, etc., and four times in the just-cited adverbial phrase "as of old"—in all, twelve times. The complementary word "new" occurs as an adverb *(eššiš* 'anew') five times, and as a verb twice—in all, seven times. Nabonidus' intentions could not be more significantly emphasized.

The central part is divided into two sections by the two occurrences of the section-introducing *inūšu* 'then,' 'at that time,' in lines 49 and 59. As in other royal inscriptions, the *inūšu* section contains the narrative about the king's activities which occasioned the composition, to which the *īnu* 'when' clause provided the background. Here the two *inūšu* clauses divide these activities into two distinct aspects of the same event.[17] The first reports on the building activities involved, and the second on the endowment of the complex and the exemptions granted the personnel.

The first clause relates yet another providential find of an ancient record. The stela first discovered was ascribed to Nebuchadnezzar I,[18] who was said to have listed the appurtenances of the high priestess on a stela representing her, a deed that we know of from no other source and which, we have suggested, may have been mentioned by Nabonidus as *fraus pia*.[19]

The ancient record described in the second part is the one which provided the link with the most ancient past. The discovery occurred when Nabonidus cleared the ruins of the ancient site of the high priestess's residence to establish the old ground plan. The two lines which describe the landscape of ruins are, in spite of their brevity, a welcome addition to the rare and sparse descriptions of nature that we possess:

> At that time Egipar, the holy precinct, wherein the rites of the high priestess used to be carried out,
> was an abandoned place and had become a heap of ruins,
> palm trees and orchard fruit were growing in its midst.

It was upon cutting down these trees and removing the rubble that Nabonidus could recognize the ancient foundations in which the inscription had been laid. The author of this inscription was En-ane-du, a former high priestess, herself daughter of a king—Kudur-Mabuk—and also sister of a king, the powerful Rīm-Sin of the Larsa dynasty, here called "king of Ur."[20]

This very inscription—or another ancient examplar of it—came to light again in this century.[21] It is written in Sumerian though its linguistic features betray that it was composed by scribes for whom Sumerian was a second language. Nabonidus describes its contents—in Akkadian—closely following the wording of the Sumerian text, as in the cemetery's designation as "the sleeping place of the old high priestesses," and he repeats En-ane-du's claim when he adds (line 58) "I made the house into a secure place." For the rest, he summarizes in four lines En-ane-du's lengthy foundation document, singling out only her name (line 45), her relation to the two ancient rulers (line 46), and the fact that she restored Egipar and built a wall around the cemetery (lines 47-48), two activities that En-ane-du herself lists in two sections, each introduced by $u_4.ba$ 'then,' which corresponds to the Akkadian adverb *inūšu*. The other "inscriptions of old earlier kings" that Nabonidus claims to have discovered in the ruins cannot be identified today, since Nabonidus avoids mentioning the names of these "old earlier kings" or citing the wording of the texts; he may here refer to bricks inscribed with short dedicatory inscriptions of the Kassite king Kurigalzu.[22]

It is, however, En-ane-du's foundation document that provides Nabonidus with the direct link to the ancient institution. Nabonidus can now proceed with the rebuilding of the holy precinct as a residence for his own daughter, and install her with the proper ceremonies, endowing the complex with the estates necessary for furnishing the regular offerings; he also rebuilds the cemetery wall built by En-ane-du, making his daughter's residence—he closes this section of the report—into a secure place.

The next section, the second *inūšu* clause (lines 59-72), describes how Nabonidus provided for the offerings to the Moon god and his consort Ningal and how he exempted the temple personnel from every extraneous obligation so that they could fulfill their duties in the maintenance of the cult.

The list of the temple personnel takes up six lines; the first and the last give a summary description, "the consecrated personnel of the temples" and "the collegium of priests here enumerated"; of the middle four lines the first two consist of a mere enumeration of titles, five titles in each line, but the other two expand on the titles with the descriptive phrases "who perform lamentations" and "who gladden the gods' hearts." The titles themselves are, in keeping with the emphasis on the revival of old customs, rare and archaic terms, mostly borrowed from Sumerian; even those that designate common professions, such as the brewer or the cook, are written with uncommon Sumerian word-signs.

The final part is the prayer for the god's blessing. Prayers at the end of votive inscriptions ask for the god's favor in return for the pious deeds, especially the building of temples, that are the objects of the king's dedication; they ask that the dedicated building endure forever. In this inscription Nabonidus dedicates not a building—although part of the inscription also relates the rebuilding of the holy precinct—but his daughter. Fittingly, therefore, the prayer asks that his daughter be granted good health and finding favor with the gods.[23]

This final part too, like the first, is divided into three sections. In the first section (lines 73-79) the prayer does not yet address the Moon god; it speaks of him in the third person. In the second section (80-83) there comes a brusque change to a direct address to the Moon god; the last section, the very end of the inscription, contains Nabonidus' prayer for his daughter.

The prayer is filled with analogical images and metaphors, more, perhaps, than we can readily understand. The first title given to the Moon god in line 73 is "Lord of the crown," an epithet that refers to the full moon that the term "crown" designates; the king asks that he make firm the royal crown on his head (line 79). Since the Moon had given a sign (*ittu,* lines 7 and 10), the king asks, repeating the word *ittu,* that the god bring him good signs every month (line 78). The Moon god holds a signal (*ṣaddu,* line 6) for all men; the king asks that he be favored to behold a favorable signal at every new moon (line 82), the phenomenon described in the phrase "when you renew yourself." While the ever-repeated marvel of the moon renewing itself every month hardly ever fails to be mentioned in hymns and prayers to the Moon god, it is of course not the moon but the sun who is the light-giving god par excellence. In this prayer, however, and pointedly in the very first line, the epithet *nūr tenēšēti* 'light of mankind' is applied to Sin (line 73).

The prayer's second part ends with the petition that the god's spouse, Ningal, speak to her husband in favor of the king. Ningal, who has been mentioned thus far only in the second section of the central part (lines 59, 62, and 72) and at the very end of the first part (line 48), and was always paired with Sin, here receives a separate appeal, so that the final prayer for his daughter's welfare can now be addressed to both Sin and Ningal.

In this inscription Nabonidus uses the device of articulating the text by means of the particles *īnu* 'when' and its counterpart *inūšu* 'then'—a pattern modeled on Sumerian dedicatory inscriptions—to foreground the main topics. Each articulation point—each particle—introduces a key element. The first word, *īnu*, is followed by the Sumerian name of the Moon god, Nanna(r). Each of the two occurrences of *inūšu* immediately precedes a proper name too. The first is followed by Egipar, the name of the sacred areas that Nabonidus restored for the residence of the high priestess; the second—by means of a grammatical device that permits the inversion of a genitive construction—by the names of the gods whom Nabonidus' daughter will serve: Sin and Ningal. The last part, not introduced by any particle, begins directly with the name Sin. Thus three of the four parts begin with the name of the Moon god; the Sumerian name, Nannar, in the first, the Akkadian, Sin, in the last two. In contrast, the name of the king himself does not occur in a prominent place and, as we have pointed out, appears as object of a preposition only. Even the name of the designated priestess, En-nigaldi-Nanna, is first introduced simply as the name given to the otherwise unnamed princess; only in the final prayer is this name placed in a syntactically prominent position.

The high priestess with the Sumerian name En-nigaldi-Nanna would serve the Moon god, inaugurating, so Nabonidus hoped, a renaissance of the cult at Ur, a renaissance that he was so providentially enabled to bring about. The authority of the past so emphasized in this inscription would also lend Nabonidus a support that in the end failed him when he faced the threat of the armies of Cyrus. His *apologia* is yet to be written. From Babylonia only tendentious literature directed against him survives, and the alien and unnatural behavior chastised in these writings resulted in his portrait as mad king in the Book of Daniel, under the name Nebuchadnezzar, his predecessor, with whom Nabonidus' figure became conflated.[24]

NOTES

1. G. Goossens, "Les recherches historiques à l'époque néo-babylonienne," RA 42 (1948) 149-159, and passim in the literature dealing with this period.

2. See the texts cited in notes 9 and 13.

3. From among the abundant literature on this topic see especially W. Röllig, "Erwägungen zu neuen Stelen König Nabonids," ZA 56 (1964) 218-260, who also quotes much of the relevant literature.

4. For the history of Ur in the centuries intervening see J. A. Brinkman, Or. NS 38 (1969) 310-348.

5. Penelope Weadock, Iraq 37 (1975) 112; see also the article cited in note 4, especially pp. 333f. and p. 334 notes 1 and 2.

6. P.-R. Berger, *Die neubabylonischen Königsinschriften* (= AOAT 4/1), Kevelaer: Butzon and Bercker 1973, counts five parts, assigning, as elsewhere, separate status to the section beginning with "I" or "As for me" (line 11).

7. S. Langdon, *Building Inscriptions of the Neo-Babylonian Empire* (Paris 1905), pp. 9ff.; idem, *Die neubabylonischen Königsinschriften* (= VAB 4), Leipzig, 1912, pp. 5ff.; Sigmund Mowinckel, "Die vorderasiatischen Königs- und Fürsteninschriften, eine stilistische Studie," *Eucharisterion*. Studien zur Religion und Literatur des Alten und Neuen Testaments Hermann Gunkel zum 60. Geburtstage ... Göttingen: Vandenhoeck and Ruprecht 1923, pp. 278-322.

8. *Iqqur īpuš* (= The Babylonian Calendar) § 73. The correlation between this omen and the eclipse under Nabonidus was first observed by Paul Koschaker, *Rechtsvergleichende Studien* ... (1917) 232f., who had at his disposal a translation of Nabonidus' report by his teacher H. Zimmern; it has been commented upon by, among others, J. Nougayrol, RA 40 74; Labat Calendrier §73 note 6. The date of the eclipse has been established as September 26, 554 B.C. by Hildegard Lewy, ArOr 17/2 (1949) p. 50 note 105. Of the two texts cited by these authors only the second (K. 3768+ = ACh Sin 25) belongs to *Enūma Anu Enlil* Tablet XVII; the other belongs to the series *iqqur īpuš*.

9. The consultation of the celestial omen series is mentioned in another report of the same event published by W. G. Lambert, AfO 22 (1968/69) pp. 1ff., iii 2f.; cf. P.-R. Berger, op. cit. pp. 71f., and Lambert, Proc. of the Fifth Seminar for Arabian Studies (London 1972) pp. 53-64.

10. Elsewhere, too, Nabonidus quotes from a hemerology: *ina Tašrītu* UD.17.KAM *ūmu Sin immaggar piširšu* 'on the 17th of Tašrītu (= the seventh month), which is explained as the day when Sin is favorable' is a quote from the standard hemerologies which characterize the 17th of Tašrītu as *Sin amēla imangar* 'Sin is favorable to the man,' see Röllig, ZA 56 253 note 100.

11. This is documented by a text from Mari (CRRA 2 46f.), see A. L. Oppenheim, *DSB* XV 659 note 116.

12. As is also recounted in other inscriptions of Nabonidus. A report on a "checked" extispicy *(apqidma)* followed by a third extispicy which was favorable,

and a second query *(ašnīma)* aimed at eliciting an answer to a differently worded question concerning the fashioning of a crown for Šamaš, which was answered favorably, is found in his inscription No. 7 ii 2-9. No. 3 mentions two extispicies *(ašnīma alput pu[hāda])* in ii 45; and in No. 8 the extispicy may have been performed to confirm a dream.

13. Another reference to his daughter's installation which is worded exactly like lines 24-25 gives as reason only the request of Sin: "I reverently heeded the wish that he has expressed to me, I did not withhold his wish from him but agreed to his command." RA 11 109ff. (in Berger's nomenclature Cyl. II, 5) ii 11ff.

14. For these priestesses see E. Sollberger, AfO 17 (1954-56) 23-29.

15. The incident is related in similar terms, but omitting the qualifying "ancient," in the parallel report AfO 22 4 iii 5ff.

16. While the phrase *kīma labīrimma eššiš ēpuš* occurs elsewhere in the inscriptions of Nabonidus, e.g., RA 11 111 ii 4 cited in note 13, nowhere else does it occur with the same frequency.

17. Other inscriptions that contain two *inūšu* sections refer to two activities, such as the rebuilding of different temples, see Berger, op. cit. pp. 57f.

18. Nebuchadnezzar I advises Nabonidus also in the dream reported in his text No. 8, see Oppenheim, Dream-book p. 250 No. 13 and pp. 203ff. For identification with Nebuchadnezzar I and not II see Berger, op. cit. p. 63.

19. The only other mention of a providential discovery of an ancient stela that enables the fashioning of a new divine statue is in BBSt. No. 36 iii 19-25; see Brinkman PKB 183ff. and RA 70 (1976) 183f. The terms referring to the features recorded on the stela are practically the same in both texts: *ṣalmu, simātu,* and *šiknu*. In fact, the stone tablet of king Nabû-apla-iddina which records this providential discovery was handed down over the centuries (from the ninth century B.C.) down to the time of Nabopolassar, the first ruler of the Chaldean dynasty, who preceded Nabonidus only by about fifty years. Nabopolassar wrote his own inscription on a clay mold of this tablet, confirming the endowment of the temple made by Nabû-apla-iddina.

20. En-ane-du was most likely the last such high priestess; see Sollberger, AfO 17 26. "Enanedu est la dernière grande-prêtresse de Nanna pour la période qui nous occupe. Peut-être faut-il même dire simplement *la* dernière, car il semble bien que les très rares titulaires du poste que l'on connaisse entre Enanedu et la célèbre fille de Nabonide doivent leur situation à des restaurations artificielles et d'ailleurs éphémères du vieux culte, plutôt qu'au maintien ininterrompu de la tradition."

21. It was first published by C. J. Gadd, Iraq 13 (1951) 27ff.; a more recent and up-to-date translation is given in Sollberger-Kupper, IRSA pp. 209f., No. IVB14h.

22. Weadock, Iraq 37 111; Brinkman, Or. NS 38 315ff.

23. Apart from good health, authority, and finding favor with Sin and Ningal in whatever she does, the final pious wish is for his daughter not to be guilty of cultic errors *(aj iršâ hitīti),* the same wish Nabonidus expresses for his eldest son Belshazzar (No. 4 i 23, see Berger, op. cit. p. 69, also CT 34 27 i 39f., etc.).

24. See most recently W. von Soden, ZA 70 (1981) 309f. (review of Klaus Koch, *Das Buch Daniel*).

2. ASSURBANIPAL AND THE LEGITIMATION BY THE PRESENT

In 612 B.C. Nineveh, capital of the Assyrian empire, fell to the Medes. Soon Assyria was to be totally eclipsed, after several hundred years of not political domination alone but of cultural leadership as well. The last great king of Assyria, Assurbanipal (668-627 B.C.), laid many claims to greatness. In our eyes none of his achievements is as important as his having created a royal library in Nineveh. Much of our information on scholarly and literary texts comes from nineteenth-century excavations of this library which housed not only tablets written in Assyria but also others, brought from Babylonia on Assurbanipal's orders. Assurbanipal was not, however, a collector only. He prided himself on being a literate ruler. In fact, he is the first king in Mesopotamia since the Sumerian ruler Šulgi (2094-2047 B.C.) to boast of his literary and scholarly accomplishments. The scribes who composed *res gestae* in his name emulated, if not surpassed, those of his ancestor, Sargon.

These royal *res gestae,* which may take the form of annals or votive inscriptions—the former in Assyria, the latter in Babylonia—are the only examples of sustained elevated prose from Mesopotamia, although a similar tenor is exhibited on occasion by certain types of more or less contemporary texts, such as those recording royal grants. Mostly couched as first-person narratives, they relate the king's campaigns and victories and the lavish care expended on his favorite cities and the gods' abodes. They often include narrative elements and poetic descriptions of landscapes and artifacts; they also, most importantly, speak the praise of the king and his prowess and ascribe the legitimacy of his kingship to the gods who selected and elevated him. This legitimation of the king's rule is always insisted upon, even if the dynastic succession is not in doubt.

In 1878 Hormuzd Rassam, excavating on behalf of the British in Nineveh, found a clay "cylinder"—to this day called the "Rassam Cylinder" even though a decagonal prism in reality—with the annals of Assurbanipal, the longest and best preserved of all his inscriptions.[1] Each of the ten faces of the cylinder is inscribed with, on the average, 130 lines; a transcription of one line from the cuneiform syllabic script into the Latin alphabet would contain between 20 and 50 characters, yielding for the 1303 lines of this inscription about 600 printed lines, or approximately fifteen pages.

The first 51 lines, all that I will discuss here, would take up, if printed as a continuous prose text, some 25-30 lines. I shall present their transcription in such a way that the text's compositional structure should be apparent, a structure which, as will be seen, corresponds with few exceptions to the layout of the text on the original cylinder.[2]

These first 51 lines are the introduction to the royal campaigns, which take up the remaining nine and a half faces of the prism; only the last seventy lines relate the king's building activities on the crown prince's residence, the occasion for the inscription. The text ends with a short admonition to future rulers, invoking the gods' blessings on the successor who maintains this building and remembers its builder and the gods' curses on him who fails to do so. All that precedes the report of this construction thus constitutes the justification for the king's claim to be remembered by posterity.

[1] anāku Aššur-bāni-apli binût Aššur u Ninlil
[2] mār šarri rabû ša bīt ridûti
[3] ša Aššur u Sin bēl agê ultu ūmī rūqūti [4] nibīt šumišu izkuru ana šarrūti
[5] u ina libbi ummišu ibnû ana rē'ut māt Aššur
[6] Šamaš Adad u Ištar ina pursišunu kēni [7] iqbû epēš šarrūtija
[8] Aššur-aha-iddina šar māt Aššur abu bānūa
[9] amat Aššur u Ninlil ilī tiklēšu itta'id
[10] ša iqbûšu epēš šarrūtija
[11] ina Ajari arah Ea bēl tenēšēti
[12] UD.12.KAM ūmu magru nadān akāli ša Gula
[13] ina epiš pî muttalli [14] ša Aššur Ninlil Sin Šamaš Adad
[15] Bēl Nabû Ištar ša Ninua [16] Šarrat Kidmuri Ištar ša Arba'il
[17] Ninurta Nergal Nusku iqbû
[18] upahhir nišē māt Aššur șeher u rabi
[19] ša tâmti elīti u šaplīt(i)
[20] ana nașir mār šarrūtija u arkānu [21] šarrūtu māt Aššur epēš
adê niš ilāni [22] ušazkiršunūti udannina riksāte
[23] ina hidâti rīšāte ērub ana bīt ridûti
[24] ašru naklu markas šarrūti
[25] ša Sin-ahhē-erība abi abi ālidija
[26] mār-šarrūtu u šarrūtu ēpušu ina libbišu
[27] ašar Aššur-aha-iddina abu bānūa qerebšu i'aldu
[28] irbû ēpušu bēlūt māt Aššur
[29] gimir malkī irdû kimtu urappišu
[30] ikșuru nišūtu u salātu
[31] u anāku Aššur-bāni-apli qerebšu āhuz nēmeqi Nabû
[32] kullat țupšarrūti ša gimir ummâni [33] mala bašû ihzīšunu ahīț
[34] almad šalê qašti rukkub sīsê narkabti șabāt ašâte
[35] ina qibīt ilāni rabûti
ša azkura nibīssun [36] adabbuba tanittašun
iqbû epēš šarrūtija

³⁷zanin ešrētišun ušadgilu panūa
³⁸kīmūa ētappalu bēl ṣaltija ināru gārēja
³⁹zikaru qardu narām Aššur u Ištar
⁴⁰liplīpi šarrūti anāku
⁴¹ultu Aššur Sin Šamaš Adad Bēl Nabû ⁴²Ištar ša Ninua Šarrat Kidmuri
⁴³Ištar ša Arba'il Nergal Nusku
⁴⁴ṭābiš ušēšibuinni ina kussî abi bānija
⁴⁵Adad zunnēšu umaššera Ea upaṭṭira nagbēšu
⁴⁶hamiš ina ammati še'u išqu ina absinnišu
⁴⁷ērik šūbultu $\frac{5}{6}$ ammat
⁴⁸ešēr ebūri napāš Nisaba
⁴⁹kajān ušahnabu gipārū
⁵⁰sippāti šummuha inbu būlu šutēšur ina tālitti
⁵¹ina palēja nuhšu ṭuhdu ina šanātija kummuru hegallu

¹I am Assurbanipal, created by Aššur and Ninlil,
²the crown prince from the House of Administration,
³⁻⁴whose name Aššur and Sin, the Lord of the Crown, from of old proclaimed for kingship,
⁵and whom in his mother's womb they created for the shepherdship of Assyria.
⁶⁻⁷Šamaš, Adad, and Ištar promised my exercising the kingship through their reliable oracles.
⁸Esarhaddon, king of Assyria, my own father,
⁹heeded the orders of Aššur and Ninlil, the deities in whom he put his trust,
¹⁰by which they promised him that I will exercise the kingship.
¹¹In the month of Ajaru, the month of Ea, lord of mankind,
¹²on the twelfth day, a favorable day, (the day) for offering food to Gula,
¹³⁻¹⁷following the noble command that Aššur, Ninlil, Sin, Šamaš, Adad, Bēl, Nabû, Ištar of Nineveh, the Queen of Kidmuri, Ištar of Ninurta, Nergal, (and) Nusku had given
¹⁸he convened the people of Assyria young and old,
¹⁹from coast to coast,
²⁰⁻²¹for protecting my crown-princeship and—afterward—my exercising the kingship over Assyria
²¹⁻²²he made them pronounce a sworn agreement and established a binding treaty.
²³Amidst rejoicing and merrymaking I entered the House of Administration,
²⁴an artfully constructed place, the node of the kingdom,
²⁵wherein Sennacherib, father of the father who engendered me,

²⁶exercised the crown-princeship and kingship,
²⁷in which Esarhaddon, my own father, was born,
²⁸grew up, exercised the rule over Assyria,
²⁹ruled all foreign kings, extended the family,
³⁰and brought together relatives from sword side and distaff side;
³¹and in it I myself, Assurbanipal, learned the wisdom (whose patron is) Nabû,
³²⁻³³the entire scribal art; I examined the teachings of all the masters, as many as there are.
³⁴I learned to shoot the bow, to ride horses and chariots, to hold the reins.
³⁵⁻³⁶By the pronouncement of the great gods
whose names I invoked, whose praises I speak
—(who) had promised that I would exercise the kingship—
³⁷they entrusted me with the care of their sanctuaries,
³⁸answered my opponents in my stead, defeated my enemies.
³⁹I am an accomplished man, beloved by Aššur and Ištar,
⁴⁰descendant of royal lineage.
⁴¹⁻⁴³After Aššur, Sin, Šamaš, Adad, Bēl, Nabû, Ištar of Nineveh, the Queen of Kidmuri, Ištar of Arbela, Nergal, (and) Nusku
⁴⁴graciously seated me on the throne of my own father,
⁴⁵Adad released his rains, Ea opened his springs;
⁴⁶the barley in its furrow grew five cubits high,
⁴⁷the ear grew five-sixths of a cubit long,
⁴⁸(there was) thriving of crops, abundance of grain;
⁴⁹the grasslands grew luxuriantly at all times,
⁵⁰the orchards were bedecked with fruit, the cattle were thriving in offspring;
⁵¹during my reign prosperity and plenty, during my years bountiful produce was amassed.

Assurbanipal's first word is "I": "I am Assurbanipal." This introduction is typical of those narratives, real or legendary, which purport to be self-presentations of a king or of a god, and indeed defines a group of texts that may be subsumed under the term "autobiography." Royal annals and votive inscriptions otherwise begin with a name: the name of the king, if not directly that of the god who is addressed. The use of the pronoun "I" *(anāku)* by Assurbanipal here as in other inscriptions permits him not only to dwell on his achievements and personal accomplishments but also to shift the emphasis from the dedicatory object to the human intelligence and will that brought forth the events and monuments related and described on it; his predecessors' inscribed tablets and artifacts often begin with the phrase "property of King so-and-so," thus focusing on the material object instead of on the author. The initial "I" also serves to link the inscription's beginning to its end and thus to give it a unity when Assurbanipal some 1200 lines later returns to his achievements with this same pronoun *anāku* "I."

No human intelligence and will can achieve its goal, of course, without the will of the gods. The self-presentation is therefore immediately followed by the statement that all that is to follow has been sanctioned, ordained, or specifically requested by the gods.

This text, however, is more than a standard royal inscription in which it suffices to state the king's name and ancestry and acknowledge the bounties that the gods have bestowed upon him or the victories they helped him to attain. Here Assurbanipal, in relating how, after his campaigns narrated on the ten faces of the cylinder, he rebuilt the House of Administration, is intent on legitimating his own succession to his father's throne, a succession that, as we have recently learned, was not his hereditary due. His father Esarhaddon solemly proclaimed him crown prince designate of Assyria over his older brother Šamaš-šum-ukin and installed him in the crown prince's official residence, the House of Administration. We know this from a document that imposes an oath of loyalty to Assurbanipal on vassals of Assyria, the so-called Vassal Treaties of Esarhaddon.[3]

Accordingly, immediately after identifying himself, Assurbanipal adds his two most important claims to the throne. First, he states that he is the creature of the national gods of Assyria, Aššur and his consort Ninlil, and, second, that he is "the crown prince from the House of Administration," that is, one who was proclaimed as crown prince designate in his father's lifetime and given this House of Administration as residence. The next two clauses (lines 3-7) elaborate on his calling by specifying how it was ordained by the gods. Whereas the second clause lists the deities Šamaš, Adad, and Ištar in their usual order, in the first only two of the elder gods figure: Aššur himself and the Moon god, Sin. The epithet given to the Moon god, "Lord of the Crown,"—normally his title at full moon, as "crown" is the name of the moon disk—is a deliberate double entendre: Lord of the Crown also means "he who has power of disposal of the crown"; the chosen epithet is no mere filler but serves a definite function in the king's legitimation. This interpretation is supported by the unusual prominence given to Sin next to Aššur; Enlil and Ea, the two gods who normally precede Sin in similar enumerations, are altogether omitted. Assurbanipal's calling by Aššur and Sin is expressed in two clauses exhibiting the syntactic parallelism favored by Near Eastern poetry: from of old // in his mother's womb; have proclaimed // have created; for kingship // for the shepherdship of Assyria.

The three gods listed in the second clause decreed that Assurbanipal should rule "through their reliable oracles," that is, through portents communicated by omens and through oracles delivered by the deities' spokesmen. Šamaš and Adad elsewhere too form a pair as the patron gods of extispicy—divination from the entrails of the sheep—and were invoked, from the early second millennium on, by the haruspex before he examined the sheep's liver in order to obtain a reliable omen. We are not told here what the portent given by Šamaš and Adad was, nor what was the oracle given by Ištar. Ištar's mention here is not simply part of the usual sequence, following that of Sin, her father, and Šamaš, her brother. Her role as dispenser of oracles is part of the religious beliefs of the Neo-Assyrian period. Through men and women ecstatics she has delivered oracles for King Esarhaddon and would continue to do so for King Assurbanipal. Yet Ištar's dispensing of special favors to rulers is part of an age-old tradition, going back to the third millennium B.C. when kings began to call themselves "favorites of Ištar"; Sargon of Akkad, the founder of the Akkad dynasty (ca. 2300 B.C.) not only includes this epithet in his titulature but also explicitly speaks of Ištar's love for him in the autobiographic poem (though most likely apocryphal) we know under the title *The Birth Legend of Sargon.* Assurbanipal's own great-grandfather, who in 722 B.C. founded the dynasty we call Sargonid, assumed this very name (Šarru-kīn, meaning "legitimate king"), harking back to his famous predecessor in the third millennium, when he usurped the Assyrian throne; it is with him, perhaps, that Ištar as protectress of kings reappears in Mesopotamian royal ideology.[4]

The divine approval of his succession thus established, Assurbanipal proceeds to narrate the actual historical event, the proclamation of his crown-prince status by the ruling king, Esarhaddon. It is described in lines 8-22, a complex period which begins by naming Esarhaddon and ends with the word "treaty." In contrast to the preceding short, parallel sentences, this period consists of three clauses of uneven length, each weighted with a string of epithets and embedded relative clauses and rendered solemn by enumerations of names of deities. The gods named in the first clause (lines 8-10) are again the two national gods, Aššur and Ninlil, qualified as "the gods in whom he [Esarhaddon] puts his trust"; they are mentioned here, as in the very first line, to emphasize that Esarhaddon acted upon the orders of Assyria's gods in installing Assurbanipal as crown prince. Accordingly the key phrase, *iqbû epēš šarrūtija,* "promised that I will exercise the kingship," first used in line 7, recurs in line 10; it recurs a third and last time in line 36, subsuming under the general designation "great gods" the previously named gods, but here with the emphasis on Assurbanipal's own devotion to them, so as to express that it was his gratitude and piety that earned him the gods' continuing favor.

The middle clause (lines 11-19) starts with a leisurely series of complements: a temporal clause (11-12) and an instrumental clause (13-17), both introduced by *ina,* a preposition meaning "in" as well as "through." The first specifies the date: the twelfth of the month of Ajaru. The names of both the month and the day are given attributes in the form of quotes from hemerologies—calendars identifying favorable and unfavorable days. The quotes insist on the propitious nature of the day (*ūmu magru* "a favorable day") but also add other epithets not apparently connected with the occasion, to describe the month of Ajaru as the month placed under the protection of "Ea, lord of mankind," and the twelfth day as the day on which food offerings are presented to the goddess Gula, two deities who do not appear in the enumerations that follow and who evidently play no role in determining the royal succession. The embellishments added to the date impart to it a solemnity, both religious and learned, by drawing upon the calendar literature; this device was used, as we have seen, by Nabonidus as well.

The citations from the hemerologies, extending over two lines, slow the pace of the sentence, and the meandering list of divine names taking up four lines in the instrumental clause does so even more. The similar list in lines 41-43 omits the names of Ninlil and Ninurta but keeps the same sequence; the list is, in fact, substantially the same as the one that heads the Vassal Treaties, the imposition of which is here described, yet the fact that it diverges slightly from the Treaties indicates that it was not copied from it.[5]

After this long lead-in Esarhaddon's action—"he convened all the inhabitants of Assyria from coast to coast"—is suddenly foregrounded in line 18 by the placement of the verb *upaḫḫir* 'he convened' in the marked, initial position that both gives emphasis to the event and contrasts with the pattern of the two previous sentences. The last clause (lines 20-22) which these involved clauses have been leading up to states the decisive act: the administration of the loyalty oath to the people of Assyria and to the chiefs of territories under Assyrian suzerainty, having them swear to protect "the crown-princeship" of Assurbanipal and—with a euphemism avoiding the mention of Esarhaddon's eventual death—"afterward" his "exercising the kingship over Assyria." We now see why the accompanying circumstances—the month, the day, the gods presiding over the treaty—have been described in this solemn, measured pace; although nowhere is there an explicit reference to the particulars of the oath-taking ceremony and the many detailed provisions of the treaty (perhaps to avoid bringing to mind the irregularity surrounding Assurbanipal's designation as crown prince), the solemnity of the event has left its mark on the narrative recalling it.[6]

In the next section (lines 23-40) Assurbanipal describes his youth and education in the House of Administration which he "entered amidst rejoicing and merrymaking"—a prerogative obviously conferred on him as Esarhaddon's designated successor, though he leaves this causal connection unsaid. This House of Administration had served, he takes pains to explain, as royal residence of his grandfather Sennacherib and as birthplace and royal residence of his father Esarhaddon. The fine distinction between the statements that in it Sennacherib "exercised the function of crown prince and the kingship" whereas Esarhaddon "was born, raised, and exercised the rule over Assyria" is difficult to assess, since the throne was seized by Esarhaddon after his brothers had murdered their father Sennacherib.[7] The mention of Esarhaddon's birth in this very House of Administration may be an attempt to place emphasis on the legitimate succession of Assurbanipal's father himself, who expressly claimed the right to the throne as the heir chosen by his father Sennacherib. From that royal residence, Assurbanipal continues, Esarhaddon ruled his empire, a rule represented as hegemony over "all foreign kings" abroad and the attitude of a paterfamilias at home. The latter characterization, couched in the unusual terms "extended the family, brought together relatives from sword side and distaff side," probably contains precise allusions or literary echoes; only the first half can be identified as an allusion to Hammurapi, the famous lawgiver king of the First Dynasty of Babylon in the 18th century B.C., since we know from a late list that the name Hammurapi was interpreted as *Kimtu-rapaštu,* 'extensive family.'

Assurbanipal's education—of which he often boasts—included both book learning and martial skills. He studied "the entire scribal art" and "examined the teachings of all the masters," phrases that regularly appear in the colophons of the tablets he collected in his library at Nineveh. The range of his skills, such as the ability to read and write even the most abstruse forms of cuneiform and to use arithmetical tables, are often detailed in the just-mentioned colophons and in other reports of his achievements. While his claims may contain a pardonable dose of exaggeration, it appears that Assurbanipal indeed knew how to read: in a number of reports addressed to him, technical and rare (and sometimes not so rare) words are glossed (spelled out with simple syllables), undoubtedly to enable him to read these communications himself.[8]

His training in physical dexterity consisted in learning the skills of the charioteer, that is, to drive a chariot on hunt and in war and to wield bow and arrow, accomplishments that he had depicted in reliefs on the walls of his palace and which earned him the Biblical fame of "Nimrod, a mighty hunter before the Lord."[9]

Assurbanipal does not fail to attribute his accomplishments and successes to the will and aid of the gods. Because he acted as a god-fearing person—always invoking the gods and speaking their praises—the great gods have entrusted him with the task of providing for their sanctuaries and, in return for his piety, took it upon themselves to stand against Assurbanipal's adversaries. Here Assurbanipal does not claim for himself any of the military prowess he will describe in the remaining part of this cylinder, but credits the gods alone for acting "in his stead"; he is content with listing his learning, his skills, and his piety. He sums up his self-presentation by stressing solely what is important for his legitimation (lines 39-40): he is an accomplished man, favored by Aššur and Ištar, and of long royal lineage.

As befits the reign of a king chosen and favored by the gods, Assurbanipal's reign was an era of prosperity. This is the last topic he addresses in the preamble. Again avoiding any mention of Esarhaddon's death, he states that after the gods—enumerated in line 41 in the same sequence as in lines 13-14 though with the omission of Ninlil and Ninurta— had seated him on the throne of his father, a golden age set in. This is a topos of Mesopotamian literature that turns up in specific genres, such as omen texts and prophecies, in which *Heilszeiten*—blessed times—are associated with certain rulers and their opposite, *Unheilszeiten,* with others. Characteristic of general peace and prosperity are stable or low prices; royal pride in fair prices dates back a thousand years earlier to the Old Babylonian period and even beyond. Old Babylonian law codes and royal decrees promulgate such prices; whereas Hammurapi regulates only wages, somewhat earlier royal decrees, such as the Laws of Eshnunna, also regulate the price of grain, oil and other fats, wool, and copper. In another recension of his annals (Cylinder B i 27-38) Assurbanipal combines the poetic description of the golden age of this preamble with precise details on the yields of the fields and the prices of essential commodities.

In a later passage of this cylinder (column ix 46-52) Assurbanipal returns to the topic of abundance in describing how cheaply camels were to be had after he took "countless" camels as booty from Arabia. The fascination of Mesopotamian rulers with the camel, not native to the region and encountered only on foreign campaigns, is comparable to that of the Greeks and Romans with the elephant. In this cylinder Assurbanipal boasts that he "distributed camels as if they were sheep" to the people of Assyria, and that even in the interior of the land camels could be bought on the market for less than a shekel[10] or "in exchange for a . . . of the woman tavern keeper's, a jug of beer of the brewer's, or a basket of vegetables[11] of the gardener's." A hundred years later Nabonidus, following the style and imagery not of his Babylonian predecessors, as was his wont, but of Assurbanipal (at whose court his father possibly grew up), unites the two topoi by introducing the description of prosperity with the words Assurbanipal uses in line 45: "Adad released his rains, Ea opened his springs" (adding to this quote from Assurbanipal that these two gods did so upon the command of Sin, thus ascribing to the Moon god, to whom he was especially devoted, ascendancy over the other gods), and illustrating the resulting plenty by giving the prices of barley, dates, oil, cress, wool, some other commodity (probably copper), and wine. Barley, oil, and wool were the basic necessities for subsistence; they are given out in Babylonia as rations and as payments for various services. Dates, added by Nabonidus, were an essential dietary supplement (for sugar) and in Neo-Babylonian times also served as raw material for a fermented "beer" in addition to the beer made from malt. The mention of wine, properly included in Assurbanipal's list since the northern regions had viticulture, seems to be calque in Nabonidus's list, for Babylonia, in the south, was not a wine-growing region.[12] Assurbanipal's fondness for this topos is shown, in addition to the references in his annals, in a hymn in praise of him[13] which lists the wondrously cheap prices for barley, oil, and wool.[14]

The argument for the literary character of this closing section (lines 45-51) of the preamble rests not only on the parallels adduced from inscriptions of Assurbanipal and of other kings, or even on the fact that we find ourselves in a Land of Cockaigne where "the barley in its furrow grew five cubits high, the ear grew five-sixths of a cubit long," but also on the diction of these last lines. Line 48 consists of two compounds: "thriving of crops, abundance of cereals," recalling similarly phrased omen apodoses predicting plenty, rather than of two subject-predicate clauses. The three clauses of the next two lines vary the word order (adverb—predicate—subject; subject—predicate—object; subject—predicate-complement) and none ends with the predicate, as they might in a more prosaic word order. The final line exhibits not only parallelism in its two parts but also the extremely rare and therefore highly marked syntactic construction (the rhetorical device called zeugma or adiunctio) in which a centrally or eccentrically placed verb serves as predicate to several subjects; the predicate "was amassed," placed in penultimate position, applies not only to "bountiful produce" that follows it but also to "prosperity and plenty" that closes the first half of the line.

This highly marked line, as much as the ruling on the tablet, divides the preamble discussed here from the narration of Assurbanipal's campaigns that follow. After almost twelve hundred lines of annalistic narrative, the House of Administration is reintroduced as the object of his building activity at home. The occasion for rebuilding the crown prince's residence may have been Assurbanipal's intention to install a son there; he may have been preparing to perpetuate this symbolic act of dynastic succession even as the Medes were threatening Assyria's frontiers. The rebuilding of the House of Administration that he was chosen to occupy in his father's lifetime upon the orders of the gods and the concurrence of the people and the vassals of Assyria serves him as the opportunity to insist on his own legitimate claim to the Assyrian throne.

NOTES

1. Published in transliteration and German translation by M. Streck, *Assurbanipal* (Leipzig, 1916), vol. 2 pp. 2ff. English translation D. D. Luckenbill,

Ancient Records of Assyria and Babylonia (Chicago: University of Chicago Press, 1927), vol. 2, pp. 291ff., § § 765-769.

2. When a clause extends over more than one line, the beginning of the new line is indicated by its raised line number.

3. D. J. Wiseman, *The Vassal-Treaties of Esarhaddon* (= *Iraq* 20 [1958]).

4. See H. E. Hirsch, "Eannatum von Lagaš und Sargon von Agade," *Studies Presented to A. Leo Oppenheim* (Chicago, 1964) 136-137.

5. The list of deities in the Treaty begins with the five planets Jupiter, Venus, Saturn, Mercury, and Mars, and the star Sirius; it adds, after Aššur, the names of the traditional supreme triad, Anu, Enlil, and Ea, and then parallels the lists in lines 14-17 and 41-42 except that it lists first the male deities, and only then the female ones, so that Ninlil as well as the two Ištars appear at the end, together with the goddesses Šerua and Bēlet-ili who replace Šarrat Kidmuri.

6. Assurbanipal's designation as crown prince is praised in a letter to Esarhaddon from the king's exorcist Adad-šumu-uṣur (ABL 595+ = Parpola LAS 129, see Parpola, LAS 2). For the steps involved in designating the crown prince and its evocation in a letter of Adad-šumu-uṣur (ABL 2) see P. Garelli, "L'état et la légitimité royale sous l'empire assyrien," in *Power and Propaganda,* ed. M. T. Larsen, (= *Mesopotamia* 7), Copenhagen, Akademisk Forlag 1979, p. 321, and Garelli, "La propagande royale assyrienne," *Akkadica* 27 (March-April 1982) 16-29, especially p. 21.

7. See S. Parpola, *Death in Mesopotamia,* ed. B. Alster (= *Mesopotamia* 8), Copenhagen, Akademisk Forlag 1980, pp. 171ff.

8. See A. Schott, ZA 44 (1938) 194-200.

9. Another recension (Prism F, edited by J.-M. Aynard, Bibliothèque de l'Ecole des Hautes Etudes, Sciences historiques et philologiques, 309e fascicule [Paris, 1957]) adds: "no king among humans, no lion among beasts escaped from my bow. I know how to wage war, I have been initiated in battle-formation and close combat." These accomplishments are usually associated with the Persians, following Herodotus' account (I 136) of their education in three things only: horsemanship and archery and truth-telling, see, e.g., Louis Robert, *Comptes-Rendus de l'Académie des Inscriptions et Belles-Lettres,* 1975, pp. 328-330.

10. Literally "one shekel, half a shekel." This curious number idiom that consists of naming first the larger, than the smaller amount, is less frequent in Babylonian than its opposite, but can be paralleled by the seed yielding fruit "one hundred, sixty, thirty" of the Parable of the Sower (Mt. 13, 8, while Mk. 4, 8 has "thirty, sixty, one hundred). (For the idiom "one shekel, half a shekel" in Neo-Assyrian, see K. Deller, WZKM 57 [1961] 41f.).

11. AHw. reads *uhir* 'weeds'; as this would be the only occurrence of this word, an error for Ú.SAR = *urqītu* 'vegetables' may be assumed, see Weippert, WO 7 46 n. 32.

12. It is possible, however, that Nabonidus lists the price of wine because in Harran, where his stele was set up, the climate permitted viticulture.

13. LKA 31; see Weidner, AfO 13 (1939-41) 250 ff.

14. In a letter by the same exorcist Adad-šumu-uṣur the prevailing prosperity is similarly described: "there are copious rains, abundant floods (and) a fine rate of exchange" (ABL 2 = Parpola LAS No. 121).

Assurbanipal and his queen relaxing in the royal park.
Relief from the North Palace of Assurbanipal at Nineveh.

Chapter II

TWO POEMS ABOUT THE NETHER WORLD

1. THE DESCENT OF IŠTAR: FROM MYTH TO NARRATIVE

The clash between gods is a frequent motif of Babylonian poems which reflect mythological conceptions, especially the clash between gods to whom mythology assigns different domains. Some poems tell about the rivalries of the gods alone; others also imply their consequences for man.

From several poems we learn of the division of the cosmos among the gods: the heavens have fallen to the lot of Anu, the subterranean waters to the lot of Ea, and the nether world to some lesser or fallen gods,[1] over whom Ereškigal is queen. The earth—and consequently man—is ruled by Enlil. Such a division, done by lot at the beginning of the Atra-hasis epic, is now known also from the recently published introduction to the Anzû story.

The motifs of these stories have their parallel in mythological tales of other cultures and in folklore. It is, however, their poetic quality that makes them more than mere raw material for the anthropologist or the historian of religion. What may have been a myth in some distant past has become, through the artifice of the poet, a literary creation. This is why, while the story line can be summarized in a few sentences, the analysis of the structure has to proceed at a more measured pace. The way in which these motifs are assembled is as important as, and to me more important than, the existence and interpretation of the motifs themselves.

Historians of religion will continue to offer varying interpretations of these stories, and philologists will continue to suggest textual improvements that may easily be crucial for such interpretations. Equal benefits may accrue from an examination of the poem's literary structure. By drawing attention to the foregrounding or emphasis given to certain parts of a poem dealing with mythological subjects a literary analysis may highlight a motif which the historian of religion can use with profit. Yet this side benefit is incidental to my aims. My juxtaposition here of the poems dealing with the nether world is meant only to compare and contrast the poetic form and the literary devices used for the underlying stories.

Two Babylonian poems have as their setting the nether world: The Descent of Ištar, and Nergal and Ereškigal. The titles are modern; the first was named by modern Assyriologists "Descent of Ištar into Hades" and in German "Ištars Höllenfahrt," names to remind us of other descents into the nether world, especially those well known from Greek mythology, and the Christian Harrowing of Hell (the Middle English poem about the *Descensus,* Christ's Descent to Hades).

Actually, the Babylonian poem has no such title; indeed, like the majority of the literary works of ancient Mesopotamia, it has no title at all. The locus of the story, the Hades or Hölle of the modern title, is called in the Babylonian poem "Great Earth"; in the Sumerian version to which this story ultimately goes back, "Land of No Return." The heroine, Ištar—in the Sumerian story Inanna—is the daughter of Sin, the moon god, and sister of the sun god Šamaš. Her own position in the sky is that of the planet Venus, the planet which, as the Mesopotamians had long known, is both the morning star and the evening star. Conceived as male when the morning star, Ištar is a war goddess; conceived as female when the evening star, she is the goddess of love and fecundity. This latter aspect is the motif exploited in the story of her descent into the nether world: as long as she is detained there, fertility on earth comes to a stop. Her father and the gods responsible for the functioning of the universe have to devise a way to bring her back.

The Babylonian poem takes the story no further. Only from a number of Sumerian stories do we learn how she was required to send a substitute for herself and how she delivered up as substitute her own lover, the shepherd Dumuzi. As, however, Dumuzi's absence from earth again puts a halt to fecundity in humans, animals, and crops, it is only when Dumuzi's sister offers to spend half of the year in the nether world in his stead that the orderly functioning of the world—fecundity and growth for half a year—is restored. It is this final motif that recurs in such myths as that of the Dying and Disappearing God, or the myth of Adonis, which spread so widely in the ancient world.

While the myth involving both Ištar and Dumuzi may have been background to the Babylonian poem, it is not told in either of its two extant exemplars. One of these (B) was found in the library of Assurbanipal in Nineveh, the other (A) at Assur, and both date from the first half of the first millennium B.C. While the Assur version is slightly earlier, redactional differences between the two are minor; these will be pointed out where pertinent. Both end, significantly, before the story could get embroiled in the further peripeties involving Dumuzi although it seems that the final thirteen lines allude to the rites surrounding the mourning for the dying god Dumuzi.

The first 126 lines of the Babylonian poem deal solely with the descent of Ištar and her return. The poem begins, however, like the Sumerian poem, with the line "To the Land of No Return, [the Great?] Earth, Ištar, Sin's daughter, set her mind (to descend)." The name Land of No

Return appears in its Sumerian form, probably as a—foreign—proper name, though the writing may conceal under the Sumerogram KUR.NU.GI$_4$.A its Akkadian translation equivalent *erṣet la târi*. Here are the first lines:

1   To the Land of No Return, [the Great?] Earth,
    Ištar, Sin's daughter, set her mind
    Yes, set Sin's daughter her mind
    To the house of darkness, the abode of Irkalla,
5   To the house which he who enters does not leave,
    To the road whose course does not turn back,
    To the house where those who enter remain deprived of light,
    Where their sustenance is dust and clay their food,
    They see no light and dwell in darkness,
10 Clothed, like birds, with wings for garments;
    Dust has settled upon door and lock.

The first line alone already sets this poem apart from other Babylonian epics and narrative poems. Their first words, as a rule, are some epithet of the hero, an epithet which in the next couplet may be extended to include the hero's name. *šar gimir dadmē* "King of all inhabited regions" is the first line of the Epic of Irra; *ša nagba īmuru* "He who has seen everything" of the Gilgameš Epic; *bin šar dadmē šūpâ narām Mami* "Scion of the king of the inhabited regions, the famous, beloved of Mami" of the Story of Anzû, whose hero is the god Ninurta. Next to these epithets the poet's voice is often heard: "(Him) I will sing" (Story of Anzû); "(Him) I will proclaim to the land" (Gilgameš). The first words of the Descent of Ištar, on the other hand, mention not the goddess whom we consider the heroine, but the nether world itself, thus in effect establishing the nether world as the protagonist of the story. The name of the nether world is introduced by the preposition *ana* 'to'; the Sumerian version, since that language operates with postpositions instead of prepositions, begins the poem with this very name, which thus is thrown into perhaps even starker relief. The same preposition *ana* introduces four further consecutive lines, 4 to 7, as the story's protagonist—its stage setting—is further and further specified.

Lines 2 and 3, which interrupt the sequence of these parallel-constructed lines, introduce the apparent protagonist, Ištar. They do so in a pair of lines in which the second is a curious inversion of the first, a somewhat jarring syntactic arrangement that the translation is intended to reflect. In other poems, such pairs of lines are usually built on the same pattern, and in fact are identical but for the fact that the second of the pair adds the hero's name to the epithet which alone appears in the first, and thereby is one word longer. Here this poetic convention is reversed: it is the first of the two lines that names the heroine, Ištar, before giving her the epithet "Sin's daughter," and the second that repeats the epithet, but not the name. The inversion, by placing the verb first, also gives syntactic prominence to the predicate which in the first line stands, as normal Akkadian word order requires, at the end of the sentence. The inversion in itself would not be so unusual since it is often used elsewhere too precisely to impart prominence and effect foregrounding; here, however, an idiom consisting of object-verb is inverted, indeed, torn apart, separated as its two elements are by the subject; thus, the reordering imparts a rondo-like effect to this couplet, as it moves from a word order of subject-object-verb to verb-subject-object.

Yet the arrangement of words in the couplet is no gratuitous game. The reordering also permits the return, in the subsequent lines, to the prepositional phrases with "to," akin to the first line; with their repetitive pattern these lines insist the more on the drabness of what they describe.

Each line adds a further feature to this Land of No Return which is painted as an unnatural domain, bereft of light and life. It is a "house of darkness"[2] with another strange, foreign name: Irkalla (line 4); it is a house that once you enter you do not leave (5); a road that, unlike other roads, leads only in one direction (6); a house that is not only dark (7, 9) but also lacks movement:

11   Dust has settled upon door and lock.

This lack of movement, this absence of escape have been suggested as much by the monotonous repetition of verses built on the same pattern, by the threefold line-initial repetition of *ana bīti* 'to the house,' by the insistence on the same words—*nūru* 'light' in lines 7 and 9, *epru* 'dust' in lines 8 and 11—as by the content of the description.

A certain flatness of diction is also manifest in the prevalence of verses with particles at the heads of the lines; the normally dominant pattern for a verse is to begin with a noun or a verb. Here, in addition to the five lines beginning with the preposition *ana* 'to,' line 8 begins with the conjunction *ašar* 'where' and the last and therefore the most marked line of the description begins with another preposition: *eli* 'upon.' The Assur exemplar (A) of the poem adds another line here, which, despite being partly broken, nonetheless permits no other restoration except a line-initial *eli: [eli . . .] šuharratu tabkat* 'Deathly silence has fallen [upon . . .].'

When Ištar arrives, according to line 12, at the entrance of this Land of No Return, the stage has thus been set. We would do well to dwell a little longer on this description of the nether world, since this description is not unique to our poem. It recurs verbatim in two other narrative poems: once in Nergal and Ereškigal, which is also set in the nether world, and again in the Gilgameš epic in a report on Enkidu's dream about the nether world. Both quotes end with the tenth line of the above-quoted poem, omitting the line "Dust has settled upon door and lock."

Such verbatim quotes—of which this passage is perhaps the longest example—play the same role in Babylonian poetry as the quotes and allusions that punctuate modern poetry; they constitute intertextual relationships, and enable the well-read modern Assyriologist to make the same linkages across the ancient poems as the ancient reader was expected to make.

In the Gilgameš Epic, the quotation begins with our line 4; it is introduced by the phrase "the dream apparition led me," thus substituting for "Ištar ... set her mind" another syntagm, not only appropriate in its context but one which permits the poet to continue with the prepositional phrase "To the house of darkness...."

In Nergal and Ereškigal we pick up the quotation, after a break on the tablet, at its sixth line, "To the road whose course does not turn back," and thus we do not know what device integrated the description of the nether world into that story. The quotation continues with lines 7 and 8, but then transposes lines 9 and 10: first comes the line "[clothed], like birds, with wings for garments," and only then "[They see no light and] dwell in darkness." In this version the description continues for three more lines; these are, however, so fragmentary that only the middle line, "[They mourn?] like doves," can be restored with any certainty. Nor can the fragmentary endings of the other two lines be reconciled with either line 11 of the Nineveh version (B) or with the additional partially preserved line of the Assur version (A) of the Descent of Ištar; this suggests that Nergal and Ereškigal introduced some innovations into the description of the nether world, a trait quite consonant with its character (see Chapter II 2).

The use of the word-for-word quotation in these two poems suggests that not only did this description of the nether world accurately reflect the Babylonians' conception of it but also that the form it was here given needed—or allowed—no further improvement. There exists, however, another version of the first eleven lines of the Descent of Ištar. While the examples so far discussed are roughly contemporary, this other version (C) is much earlier, dating from the end of the second millennium, and is appended to the end of a tablet inscribed with a poem in praise of the Assyrian king Tiglathpileser I (1114-1076 B.C.). The scribe utilized the blank space remaining at the end of the tablet to inscribe on it these few lines, perhaps as an exercise in copying or composition. While the first-millennium copies of the Descent of Ištar, Gilgameš, or Nergal and Ereškigal may indeed reflect much older compositions—as may also be the case with other literary works—the fact that one of the versions appears in three different poems whereas the other has no parallel makes it likely that the second-millennium tablet records an earlier version. A comparison will best show why the Middle Assyrian version (C) might have been abandoned in favor of a better one:

Middle Assyrian Version (C)

1   To the goddess, Mistress of the Great Earth,
    To the ištar who resides in the midst of Irkalla,
    The domain of Gingal, Mistress of the Great Earth,
    To the ištar who resides in the midst of Irkalla,
5   The house of Irkalla, whose pilgrims do not return,
    A place where no light is provided for its people,
    A place where the dead are covered with dust,
    A house of darkness—no star comes forth,
    Sin's daughter directed her attention,
10 Directed her attention and set it
    —whose pilgrims do not return.

If we disregard the last, incomplete, line, which may have been placed there having been left out by error after, for instance, line 8, we have here a ten-line section corresponding to the first nine lines of the Descent of Ištar.

This section contains the same narrative and many of the same words as the later version: "house of darkness," "light," "dust." Striking as the resemblances are, equally striking are the differences. Immediately striking is the absence of the name of the protagonist, Ištar. In the Descent of Ištar she is introduced as "Ištar, Sin's daughter" as early as the second line, and her epithet "Sin's daughter" is repeated in line 3. Here, however, the corresponding two lines appear only at the end of the section, as lines 9 and 10. Nor do these lines contain her name at all: the first uses only her epithet "Sin's daughter," and the next omits even this, filling out the rhythmic structure not by giving another name or title to the heroine but, curiously, by expanding the predicate with a synonymous verb, a verb, moreover, that has no part in the idiom "directed her attention" (Akkadian *uzunša iptēma* 'opened her ears') and that sounds as redundant in the original as in the translation (Akkadian: *iptēma uzanša ušaškin* 'Opened her ear and set [it]').

Therefore in this version the opening eight lines focus on the nether world, and are not interrupted by the introduction of Ištar as protagonist. In lieu of the visitor, it is the mistress of this realm whom we find in the first four verses. Yet her name, Ereškigal, does not appear. Rather, it is paraphrased by an Akkadian translation of the elements of this Sumerian name. Ereškigal is composed of Sumerian *ereš* 'mistress,' *ki* 'earth,' and *gal* 'great'; the name means 'Mistress of the Great Earth,' and the Akkadian translation of its components as *bēlti qaqqiri rabīti*, equally 'Mistress of the Great Earth,' is the phrase used to refer to Ereškigal in lines 1 and 3. She is characterized as "goddess" in lines 1, 2, and 4; in line 1 the word used is the generic term *iltu*—a feminine form derived from the masculine *ilu* 'god'—while in line 2 and its repetition, line 4, the word used is *ištaru*, a term often used not only as the proper name of the goddess Ištar but as a generic term for "goddess," and as such paired with the masculine generic term *ilu*. This acceptable and common usage of the term *ištaru* cannot fail to appear, in this poem whose protagonist is the goddess Ištar, as a, possibly intentional, misdirection.

Whatever the reasons for the avoidance of the name Ereškigal, its foreignness could not have been one of them since other, equally foreign, names abound in this segment. Irkalla, mentioned but once in the Descent of Ištar, here occurs three times (lines 2, 4, and 5); another name, Gingal, not otherwise known, is introduced in line 3 in the phrase that may be translated "Domain of Gingal" or "Gingal-Place." Thus the first four lines mention the Queen of the nether world twice, but avoiding her proper name, and the nether world three times, giving it two different names. The next four lines, giving the description of this strange domain, are connected by the very word Irkalla to the preceding quatrain. They describe the nether world in much the same terms and images as the corresponding section of the Descent of Ištar, yet their effect is totally different. The eight-line exposition in the Descent of Ištar dwells longer on the pall and gloom of this world than do the four lines of the Middle Assyrian version. Not only are the last three lines and the line "To the road whose course does not turn back" omitted and the line "Where their sustenance is dust and clay their food" replaced by "A place where the dead are covered with dust"—a line that makes use, though in a different way, of the image of dust—but gone also thereby are the knell-like repetitions of the words "darkness" and "dust." The description ends, startlingly, with the words "no star comes forth"; startlingly, because none of the descriptions of the nether world we know ever mentions the presence or absence of stars. This realm of darkness, where not even the stars shine, this realm of the Ištar of the night, is also here explicitly identified as the abode of the dead, with the word *mītūtu* 'the dead' in line 7. In the Descent of Ištar, this word does not occur in the description of the nether world at all, and is first introduced in line 19, and then only indirectly, as Ištar threatens to break down the gate and let the dead come up to the earth.

Nothing more is extant from the Middle Assyrian version than the few lines just commented upon: the description of the realm of the Mistress of the Great Earth and the announcement that "Sin's daughter" directed her steps toward it. This announcement, as we have seen, begins the eleven-line introduction of the Descent of Ištar.

Ištar's name is reintroduced in line 12, as the action now sets in. This line signals the opening of the story by reintroducing in a single line both key terms: Ištar, and the Land of No Return:

12   Ištar, upon arriving at the gate of the Land of No Return
13   Speaks (these) words to the gatekeeper.

It is characteristic of Babylonian epic poetry that the action is propelled forward not so much by the description of actual events as by a series of speeches, often dialogues, in which the protagonists decide what to do or instruct others what to do. Such speeches, especially the monologues, are a way of communicating the actors' thoughts[3] or practical and moral dilemmas within a linguistic and cultural framework in which the concept of thought finds no expression in the language apart from the formulation "speak to one's heart."

In this narrative poem too direct speeches outnumber narrative passages. After the initial eleven lines only 43 more lines are descriptive; 75 lines are taken up by dialogues, speeches, and monologues, and nine lines variously introduce those speeches in the same vein as and using a formula similar to lines 12-13.

This first and only really extensive speech of Ištar addresses the gatekeeper, ordering him to open the gate so that she may enter or else she will break down the door.

14   O gatekeeper, open your gate,
15   Open your gate so that I may enter.
     If you do not open the gate and I cannot enter
     I will break down the door, I will break the lock,
     I will break down the doorframe and tear out the doors,
     I will bring up the dead, they will devour the living,
20   The dead will outnumber the living.

This strangely worded request for admittance, accompanied as it is by a dire threat, not only tells something of Ištar's character, thus preparing the reader for her subsequent actions as they unfold in the Sumerian myth (and which this poem leaves untold) but also contains the implicature that an ordinary request would not gain her admittance to the nether world. Indeed, the world of the gods and the realm of Ereškigal are so separate that not even the gods can go back and forth, as we are expressly told in the second story about the nether world, Nergal and Ereškigal.

The seven lines of Ištar's speech to the gatekeeper fall into three parts. The first two lines contain her orders, the next three her threats to break down the door, and the last two describe what would result if the gate of the nether world were thrown open: the dead would come up and devour the living, the dead would outnumber the living. Twice in these last two lines the word "dead" occurs, a word that was absent, as we pointed out, from the description of the nether world and that will not recur until the very last line of the poem, which again speaks of the coming up of the dead. This final couplet of Ištar's speech thus contains an allusion, points forward, to the end of the poem.

The change of speaker is signaled, as is usual in epic texts, by a two-line formula, naming both the speaker and the person addressed:

21   The gatekeeper set himself to speak,
22   He addresses the great (lady) Ištar:

Yet his first word, the ample introductory formula notwithstanding, is an abrupt shout of "Stop!" meant to stay Ištar's hand raised ready to break down the door. Only then does he offer, in conciliatory words, to announce her to Queen Ereškigal:

23   Stop, My Lady, do not break it down!
24   Let me go and announce your name to Queen Ereškigal.

The Assur version (A) even adds the invitation "Wait inside," with "inside" referring no doubt to the gatehouse.

The next fifteen lines deal with the gatekeeper's announcing Ištar and with Ereškigal's reaction to the news of this visit.

25   The gatekeeper went in and spoke to Ereškigal:
26   'Now your sister, Ištar, in [...]
27   Who holds the great skipping-ropes, who roils the subterranean waters before Ea.'

The gatekeeper's speech is given only a single-line introduction. What he says to Ereškigal acquaints us with some further traits of Ištar. She is Ereškigal's sister—possibly to be taken in the literal sense, but possibly in the sense of equality in rank since the title "brother" or "sister" is used as a form of address in correspondence between kings of equal rank or by a king addressing a queen. The gatekeeper's reference to Ištar's roiling the subterranean waters cannot be matched by what we know of her from other sources, but she is often described as playing with the skipping-rope, especially in her aspect as deity of war.[4]

The gatekeeper does not repeat to his mistress Ištar's threats. Nonetheless Ereškigal is completely distraught.

28   As Ereškigal heard this
29   Her face grew pallid like a cut-off tamarisk,
30   Her lips turned black like a *kunīnu*-plant.

31 'What prompted her heart to (come to) me? What made her mind *inflamed* toward me?
32 'Now, shall I drink water with the Anunnaki?
33 'Shall I eat clay instead of bread? Shall I drink roiled water instead of beer?
34 'Shall I weep for the young men who left their wives?
35 'Should I weep for the young women snatched from their lovers' embrace?
36 'And for the tender baby should I weep who was sent away before its time?'

Just as Ištar's threat upon asking admittance revealed that this was no ordinary social visit to her sister, so Ereškigal's reaction to the news of Ištar at her gate implies that Ištar's arrival forebodes no good. Her immediate reaction—her face grew pallid (literally, yellow) like a cut-off tamarisk, her lips turned black (or purple) like a *kunīnu*-plant (a plant not otherwise identifiable)—is described in terms of her physical symptoms, drawing upon an imagery used elsewhere too to depict emotions, fear as well as anger. She bursts out—and note that no formula here introduces her words—with the question "What does she want of me?" Yet the sense of her question is couched in the customary poetic form of two parallel sentences, written as two hemistichs in the Nineveh examplar (B) but as a distich in the Assur exemplar (A). She then expands in five lines (in B, six in the Assur exemplar A) on her fear of the consequences of Ištar's visit. The first three sentences have their verbs in the present-future, the last three in the optative. Both formulations may be taken either as declarative sentences or as questions; in my translation I have adopted the latter alternative, using "shall" where the Akkadian uses the present-future and "should" where the Akkadian uses the optative.

In the first three questions Ereškigal expresses her fears that whatever Ištar's designs in making this trip—designs nowhere made explicit in this poem nor for that matter in its Sumerian prototype—they would result in the queen of the nether world becoming like those over whom she now rules: the dead who, as the introductory description said, eat clay, and the Anunnaki, the gods of the nether world and according to some traditions the fallen gods,[5] who—it appears from this line—drink water and not, like their queen, beer. If these lines are taken as declarative sentences instead of questions, the difference is merely stylistic; the fears of Ereškigal remain the same.

In the next three lines, however, the alternative interpretations of the thrice-repeated verb *lubki*—the Assur exemplar omits the verb in the third line—as 'Should I weep'—a question—or as 'Let me weep'—a self-exhortation—assign different attitudes to Ereškigal. If these lines are questions, Ereškigal refuses to get involved in the plight of those who people her domain. If they are self-exhortations, they may imply that she would indeed mourn the death of those whom she herself would have spared, the groom and the bride, and the child who died in infancy. Perhaps, then, she fears that Ištar, unless granted admittance, will carry out her threat and let the dead loose upon the earth so that they will indeed "devour the living" and especially those whose time has not yet come.

Whatever thoughts or feelings her questions were meant to convey, Ereškigal obviously has no choice. So she continues:

37   'Go, gatekeeper, open the gate for her.
38   'Treat her according to the ancient rites.'

What these ancient rites are we learn from the next twenty-four lines. The narrative mode returns, but only in one-line segments, to indicate the action in the briefest way; each such line is followed by two lines, the first by two lines spoken by the gatekeeper, the remaining seven by dialogues between Ištar and the gatekeeper.

39   Off went the gatekeeper, opened the gate for her.
40   'Enter, My Lady, may the land of Cutha welcome you with joy,
41   'May the palace of the Land of No Return greet you with pleasure.'
42   He led her in through the first gate and removed the great crown from her head.
43   'Why, O gatekeeper, did you remove the great crown from my head?'
44   'Enter, My Lady, such are the rites of the Mistress of the Nether World.'
45   He led her through the second gate and removed the earrings from her ears.
46   'Why, O gatekeeper, did you remove the earrings from my ears?'
47   'Enter, My Lady, such are the rites of the Mistress of the Nether World.'
48   He led her through the third gate and removed the beads from her neck.
49   'Why, O gatekeeper, did you remove the beads from my neck?'
50   'Enter, My Lady, such are the rites of the Mistress of the Nether World.'
51   He led her through the fourth gate and removed the breastplate from her chest.
52   'Why, O gatekeeper, did you remove the breastplate from my chest?'

53 'Enter, My Lady, such are the rites of the Mistress of the Nether World.'
54 He led her through the fifth gate and removed the girdle of birth-stones from her waist.
55 'Why, O gatekeeper, did you remove the girdle of birth-stones from my waist?'
56 'Enter, My Lady, such are the rites of the Mistress of the Nether World.'
57 He led her through the sixth gate and removed her bracelets and anklets.
58 'Why, O gatekeeper, did you remove my bracelets and anklets?'
59 'Enter, My Lady, such are the rites of the Mistress of the Nether World.'
60 He led her through the seventh gate and removed the sumptuous garment from her body.
61 'Why, O gatekeeper, did you remove the sumptuous garment from my body?'
62 'Enter, My Lady, such are the rites of the Mistress of the Nether World.'

The gatekeeper follows what seems to be court etiquette. He pronounces the greeting of welcome, a formula, no doubt, as the repetitive parallelism of lines 40 and 41 indicates. He then takes the visitor through the gate, but here the resemblance to a royal visit ends and the rites of the nether world take over. There is not one gate but, as we learn, seven. At each gate we pause while the gatekeeper removes some ornament with which Ištar, of royal rank herself, was bedecked. Each pause is punctuated by an exchange between Ištar and the gatekeeper, thus increasing the reader's suspense. Ištar asks why the gatekeeper removed her ornament, and each time the gatekeeper repeats the same phrase, bidding her enter, but giving no other reason for his action than "such are the rites of the Mistress of the Nether World," referring to Queen Ereškigal by this Akkadian name. The twenty-one lines, made up of seven three-line segments, are nearly identical. The only variable items are the number of the gate and the name of the finery that is taken off; the possible symbolism of these items has provoked much speculation but no interpretation that seems pertinent to this poem.[6] The passing through the seven gates is repeated, in reverse order, toward the end of the poem as Ištar leaves the nether world and her ornaments are restored to her at each gate. There the poem does not dwell at each gate; there is no dialogue between Ištar and the gatekeeper; Ištar's exit through the gates is condensed into seven lines. How different from the twenty-one-line-long section describing Ištar's entrance, and pointing up, by contrast, how it was manipulated to create suspense.

By the timeIštar has passed through the seventh gate we have come halfway through the poem, and so we are justified for having dwelt on this first part. The remainder of the story is told in a rather sketchy fashion. Three lines describe the confrontation of the two sisters. Ten lines contain Ereškigal's instructions to her attendant, or minister plenipotentiary, Namtar—whose name means "Fate"—to let loose upon Ištar a cohort of (literally, sixty) plagues. The next five lines depict how Ištar's captivity, or possibly her death, affects the world of the living: procreation and fecundity have come to a stop as matings—singling out but a few—have ceased:

63 From the very first that Ištar descended to the Land of No Return
64 Ereškigal set eyes on her and became filled with rage toward her.
65 Ištar *took no heed* but set upon her.
66 Ereškigal set herself to speak,
67 She addresses her attendant, Namtar:
68 'Go, Namtar, [..........]
69 'Let loose upon her sixty diseases [to ......] Ištar.
70 'The eye-disease upon her eyes,
71 'The arm-disease upon her arms,
72 'The foot-disease upon her feet,
73 'The heart-disease upon her heart,
74 'The head-disease [upon her head],
75 'Upon her, all of her, to [......].'
76 After Ištar, *my* lady, [descended to the Land of No Return (or: had been so beset/had been killed/was as good as dead)]
77 The bull does not mount the cow any more, the he-ass does not impregnate the jenny,
78 Nor does the young man impregnate the young woman in the streets,
79 The young man lies in his own *chamber,*
80 The young woman lies in her own *quarters.*

The three lines describing the confrontation are so laconic as if to intentionally conceal what happened. We are the more perplexed as the action that Ištar took "upon" Ereškigal is denoted by a rare and obscure word. Nor are we really told what the "sixty diseases" did to Ištar, and not only because the crucial verb "kill" or the like is lost in the breaks at the ends of lines 69, 75, and 76, but also because the poet jumps from Ereškigal's instructions to their result, without taking the time to repeat, as is normally done in a narrative poem, how these instructions were then carried out. Instead, five of the eight lines of Ereškigal's speech detail the five individual plagues that are to attack respectively her eyes, her arms, her feet, her heart, her head—no longer protected by crown, breastplate, bracelets, or anklets[7]—and thus introduce into this concise and compressed second half of the poem (as compared with its Sumerian version) one last section making use of the device of parallelism.

Not even in the next ten-line section in which Ištar's attendant, the god Papsukkal, goes to seek help from the gods in the attire of a mourner[8] do we learn what befell Ištar in the nether world; we only learn that she "has not come up" in a line (85) so simple that it either merely states the essence of the situation or is deliberately vague and possibly euphemistic.

81   Papsukkal, the attendant of the great gods, with bowed head (literally, nose), [...] face,
82   Dressed in mourning attire, wearing his hair unkempt,
82   Went *dejectedly* and wept before Sin, her father,
84   Shed his tears before king Ea:
85   'Ištar descended to the Earth and has not come up.
86   'From the very first that Ištar descended to the Land of No Return
87   'The bull does not mount the cow any more, the he-ass does not impregnate the jenny,
88   'Nor does the young man impregnate the young woman in the streets,
89   'The young man lies in his own *chamber,*
90   'The young woman lies in her own *quarters.*'

While in the Sumerian poem the quest takes Ištar's attendant—a role there filled by a goddess—to several gods in turn, this poem takes him, after only a brief allusion to his appearing before Ištar's father Sin, directly to Ea. Here the poet does not exploit the suspense that the repeated appeals for help, each turned down for one reason or another, provide in the Sumerian version. We know, and so did the poem's public, that Ea will surely provide a solution: he is full of stratagems and has on other occasions circumvented the decrees of the gods in favor of the hero, saving one from the Flood (an episode reported both in the Atra-hasīs epic and in the Epic of Gilgameš) and enabling another to enter an alien domain (Adapa seeking entrance into heaven, Nergal seeking entrance into the nether world).

Indeed, Ea is ready with a stratagem: he creates a being named Asûšu-namir, a name that means His-Rising-Is-Bright, called in version B (from Nineveh) *assinnu* and in version A (from Assur) *kulu'u*, terms variously interpreted as 'eunuch,' 'homosexual,' or, most likely, 'transvestite actor,'[9] and instructs him in how to outwit Ereškigal.

91   Ea in his wise heart devised a stratagem.

92 He created Aṣûšu-namir, an assinnu.
93 'Go, Aṣûšu-namir, set out to the gate of the Land of No Return,
94 'Let the seven gates of the Land of No Return open for you,
95 'Let Ereškigal greet you with pleasure on seeing you.
96 'After she has become cheerful and her mood has become gracious
97 'Have her swear an oath by the great gods.
98 'Lift your head and direct your attention to the waterskin.
99 "Please, My Lady, let them give me the waterskin so that I may drink water from it." '

While in the story about Adapa and in Nergal and Ereškigal Ea gives the hero specific instructions to enable him to enter heaven or the nether world, here he does not spell out how Aṣûšu-namir is to be attired, or to what ruse he should resort in order to gain admittance. The matter-of-factness of Aṣûšu-namir's admittance and welcome in the nether world as opposed to Ištar's admittance only under threat—and even then requiring a divestiture—is not meant to point up the special character of Ištar's situation by implying that, normally, access to the nether world is easy. Other stories, as we shall see, also detail the various precautions and stratagems even gods need to enter the nether world and, especially, to depart unharmed. Rather, these few lines underscore Ea's cleverness in creating this particular being who is not subject to the rules for descent into the nether world. Ea knows that Ereškigal will be so pleased to see Aṣûšu-namir that he will extract from her an oath—one interpreter suggests that it is an oath of hospitality[10]—and thus obtain from her what he wishes. Then, Ea tells Aṣûšu-namir, he is to ask for a drink from the waterskin.

The "waterskin" has puzzled commentators since heretofore the poem has made no mention of it (unless the end of line 76 is to be restored "After Ištar, *my* lady, [was turned into a waterskin]"). In the Sumerian poem Ea's messenger asks for the corpse of Ištar while the Babylonian poet avoids, as we have seen, any reference to Ištar's death (unless, again, line 76 made reference to it).

Whether the waterskin is indeed Ištar, or simply contains the water of life necessary to resurrect her, the motif used here is well known from folktales where the hero, having obtained the promise that one wish of his would be granted, asks for the only thing that he is not supposed to ask for. And that is exactly what Ereškigal says:

100 When Ereškigal heard this
101 She slapped her thigh, she bit her finger:
102 'You have asked me for something not to be asked for.'

Note that Ereškigal's reaction immediately follows Ea's instructions, as the poet skips over the expected repetition of lines 93-99, a repetition in which the instructions couched in the imperative or optative ("go," "Let the seven gates . . . open," etc.) would have been taken up line for line in the narrative past tense ("he went," "The seven gates . . . opened," etc.). The philologist must caution, however, that the seven lines expected at this point could easily have been skipped by a copyist. Ea's instructions include, in the last line, the words his messenger is to address to Ereškigal, a direct quotation that would have been identical in such a narrative counterpart; and the copyist's eye could easily have skipped the seven lines. Therefore it remains doubtful whether, even in this condensed second half, the poet omitted the narrative section intentionally, without even a hint that a repetition is to be supplied, as is sometimes given in other narrative poems by inserting the line "The messenger appeared before so-and-so" even when the expected verbatim repetition of the messenger's words is omitted, or by inserting the phrase "and so forth" indicating to the reader or performer that such repetition is to be made.

Ereškigal's reaction is again characterized by physical gestures, slapping her thigh and biting her finger, gestures which we may take as depicting her helpless anger at being bound by oath to fulfill Aṣûšu-namir's wish. That she grants the wish is again not spelled out; instead, she launches into a long and elaborate curse:

103 'Come, Aṣûšu-namir, I will curse you with a great curse
(Version A: 'Come, Aṣ-namer, I will decree for you a fate not to be forgotten, A fate not to be forgotten for all time will I decree for you')
104 'May the bread from the city's *bakers* be your food,
105 'May the jugs of the city be your drink,
106 'May the shade of the city wall be your residence,
107 'May the threshold be your sitting place,
108 'May both the drunk and the thirsting slap your face.'

The same curse that Ereškigal hurls at Ea's creature who has tricked her recurs in two separate episodes of the Epic of Gilgameš. There it is Enkidu, Gilgameš's friend and companion, who curses with the same words, first, the hierodule who seduced him and thereby took him away from the wilderness to the civilized life of the city of Uruk, and, another time, the hunter who had instigated the hierodule's coming to fetch Enkidu because Enkidu had interfered with his plying his trade.

The thrust of this curse is, as I have discussed elsewhere,[11] to condemn the object of the curse to city life, as opposed to the freedom of the non-urbanized nomad, and thus is the first occurrence in literature of the concept of the "noble savage." Such a fate alone would be dire enough for the hunter, but in the case of the hierodule, and possibly of Aṣûšu-namir, those elements of the curse which seem to indicate that not only city life, but life as an outcast even in the city is implied slant the curse in yet another direction. How the curse affects the accursed remains unknown; neither the Epic of Gilgameš nor any of the versions of the Descent of Ištar will refer again to those thus cursed; the hierodule, the hunter, and Aṣûšu-namir play no further role in the narrative.

The next actor introduced is the minister plenipotentiary of Ereškigal, the god Namtar, who was only briefly mentioned in line 67. It is he who takes over the action of the story.

109 Ereškigal set herself to speak and said
110 Addressing a word to Namtar, her minister.
111 'Go, Namtar, *knock* on Egalgina,
112 'Adorn the thresholds with coral,
113 'Bring out the Anunnaki and seat them on golden thrones.
114 'Sprinkle Ištar with the water of life and bring her into my presence.'
115 Off went Namtar, he *knocked* on Egalgina,
116 He adorned the thresholds with coral,
117 Brought out the Anunnaki and seated them on golden thrones.
118 He sprinkled Ištar with the water of life and took her along.

In this section, as expected, the four lines of Ereškigal's instructions are repeated in the narrative past, unlike Ea's instructions whose narrative counterpart was skipped over, more likely by error than by intent, as this episode shows.

Much is unclear in this episode, but it is obvious that we witness a change of scene. The scene shifts from the abode of Ereškigal, where the encounter with Aṣûšu-namir had taken place and where—at least according to the Sumerian version—Ištar transformed into a lifeless object was kept, to a place no longer muted in dust and darkness. There stands a palace called É.GAL.GI.NA, or, according to the A (Assur) recension, DI.LI.GI.NA, names unique and non-transparent (though possibly related in some fashion to the "Gingal-Place" that is one of the designations of the nether world in C, the Middle Assyrian introduction). Its thresholds are of a shining stone (most likely coral). The Anunnaki come out of the palace to sit on golden thrones—in judgment, for they are the judges of the nether world, a role that Gilgameš assumes after his death. Their presence is required for the revival of Ištar.

With Ištar's revival, the poem abruptly shifts to the return of Ištar through the seven gates she had passed upon entering. Version A (Assur) alone inserts here the clue that the vicissitudes are not yet over by raising the need for a ransom, a theme that B, the Nineveh version, defers until after the exit through the seven gates.

    (A only)   'Go Namtar, ... her.
                     'If she does not give you a ransom for herself,
                     bring her back!'
                     Namtar . . . . her.

119 He let her out through the first gate and returned to her the sumptuous garment of her body.
120 He let her out through the second gate and returned to her her bracelets and anklets.
121 He let her out through the third gate and returned to her the girdle of birth-stones of her waist.
122 He let her out through the fourth gate and returned to her the breastplate of her chest.
123 He let her out through the fifth gate and returned to her the beads of her neck.
124 He let her out through the sixth gate and returned to her the earrings of her ears.
125 He let her out through the seventh gate and returned to her the great crown of her head.

    (B only: 126 'If she does not give you a ransom for herself, bring her back to her')

Ištar's exodus through the seven gates—in reverse order, of course—is noted in the briefest way. The god who escorts her out is not named but must be Namtar (who is addressed in the Assur recension immediately before this), who presumably will not leave her until she has indeed provided a substitute for herself. But that part of the story is not told in this poem. Only the Sumerian version—reconstructed from several fragments—tells how Inanna (the Sumerian equivalent of Ištar) searches for a god who would serve as ransom for her, how she finally delivers up her husband Dumuzi to the demons who accompany her, and how Dumuzi in turn is reprieved for one half of the year as his devoted sister agrees to spend half a year in the nether world in his stead so that growth and fertility can go on for half a year.

    The Babylonian poem abruptly shifts scene, actors, and tone. The scene is not specified; it is somewhere on earth. The actors are Dumuzi and his sister Belili; and the tone is that of a lament.

127 As for Dumuzi, the lover of your childhood,
128 Bathe (him) in pure water, anoint (him) with perfume,

129 Clothe him in a splendid garment, *play for him* a lapis lazuli flute,
130 Let courtesans *sing to gladden* his heart.
131 Belili *lavished* her jewelry (on him?),
132 (So that) his lap was filled with gems.
133 She heard the wailing of/for her brother, Belili *struck* the jewelry she wore,
134 The gems with which she filled the . . . . . . ,
135 'Do not take from me my only brother!'
136 'On the day when Dumuzi comes up to me, with him will come up the lapis lazuli flute, the carnelian bracelet,
137 'With him will come up the wailers male and female,
138 'Let the dead come up and smell the incense.'

Of the two possibilities, one, that these twelve lines condense the action of the Sumerian version, namely Dumuzi's feasting among courtesans which so angers Ištar that she surrenders him to the nether world demons, the distress of his sister Belili, and the eventual (seasonal) return of Dumuzi; and the other, that we have here a description of the annual lament for Dumuzi when he has to go down to the nether world, I prefer the latter.[12] The bathing, anointing, and clothing of Dumuzi, even the women singing to him, could well describe the funeral rite. His sister Belili would then act as a mourner, but anticipate in her lament the return of Dumuzi.

This ending does not come about by default such as, for instance, running out of space on the tablet, or for some other arbitrary reason. All three exemplars on which the ending is preserved set a horizontal ruling across the tablet, thus indicating that this is in fact the end of the tablet. Both exemplars also append a colophon. If the tablet were the first of a multi-tablet series, we would expect the colophon to so indicate, as customary, by adding as catch line the incipit of the next tablet, and/or appending some conventional scribal notation to the effect that the tablet is one of a series, for example, that it is the first tablet of a named work or that it is "unfinished," or, conversely, that it is complete by adding the notation "finished."

The colophon of the Nineveh version (B)—on two exemplars—simply states that the tablet is part of Assurbanipal's library. The Assur exemplar's colophon is partially broken; still, what is preserved shows that the tablet is not given a serial number, nor is there a catch line pointing to a continuation. The notation "finished" or "unfinished" may, however, have stood at the end of one of the broken lines.

Internal criteria also point to the text being a complete whole. In this poem concerning the realm of the dead, and whose point, according to most commentators, is the confrontation of the living and the dead,[13] but which nevertheless avoids any mention of the dead except in the two lines (19-20) uttered by Ištar as a threat, it is fitting that the word "dead" should appear in the very last line, in a repetition of the very image that Ištar's threat evokes, the dead ascending to earth. In this last line, "Let the dead come up and smell the incense," the dead come up not to devour the living but to smell incense, a phrase that evokes offerings to the gods who are invited to come and smell the incense in similar, even identical, lines in other poetic works. The gods gather to smell the incense offered by the survivor of the Flood (Utnapištim in the Gilgameš Epic, Atra-hasis in the similarly named poem); they are invited to smell the incense in prayers. Therefore, this very last invitation associates the rising of the dead with a cultic occasion, to which the spirits of the dead are invited, and not with a threat to the living as Ištar would have had it.

I have suggested in connection with another Babylonian poem[14] that the fact that a number of poems are inscribed on tablets which bear some reference to some apotropaic or prophylactic ritual points to their having been read or recited in a ritual setting, even though this may have been a secondary connection. The Babylonian version of the Descent of Ištar fits in, it seems to me, with these other poems, even if we remain in ignorance about the occasion or the reason for the ritual possibly connected with it, unless of course it was, as I propose, the annual lament for the dead Dumuzi.

NOTES

1. For these fallen gods see Hans G. Güterbock, JCS 21 (1967, published 1969), 265f.

2. In Babylonian as in all Semitic poetry constructions with a genitive replace attributive adjectives; thus, "house of darkness" is equivalent to "dark house."

3. I am indebted to my colleague Johannes M. Renger for this suggestion.

4. Landsberger altogether doubts the correctness of line 27, see WZKM 56 (1960), 123 n. 44.

5. See note 1.

6. There is one word in each line describing the actions of the gatekeeper that so far has defied interpretation. Between "he let her through the ... gate" and "took off the ..." there is another word, *um-ta-ṣi*, that seems to designate some action by the gatekeeper. It does not seem likely that it is yet another synonym of "took off" (see AHw. 1498a) since this word is not repeated in Ištar's question. Rather, it would seem to refer to some gesture or attitude, possibly quite colorless, such as, for instance, "he reached out," or possibly expressing the gatekeeper's reverence or other attitude, such as "he bowed" or "he was so bold" (see Borger, BAL[2] 144)—none of these suggestions can be justified from the lexical meaning of any of several verbs that could underlie this word.

7. Among the regalia removed at the seven gates, the crown protected her head, the breastplate, her heart, the bracelets and anklets, her arms and feet. No such obvious shield for the eyes is mentioned, but it is likely that the necklace performed, as elsewhere, an apotropaic function.

8. Adapa too, when summoned to heaven before Anu, is clad in the attire of a mourner, see Chapter II, Part 2.

9. See Anne D. Kilmer, "How Was Queen Ereškigal Tricked?" *Ugarit-Forschungen* 3 (1971) 299-309, esp. p. 300.

10. Ibid., esp. p. 304.

11. "City Bread and Bread Baked in Ashes," *Languages and Areas: Studies Presented to George V. Bobrinskoy,* University of Chicago, 1967, pp. 117-120.

12. Similar is the interpretation of Jean Bottéro, Ecole Pratique des Hautes Etudes, IVe section, sciences historiques et philologiques, Annuaire 1971/1972, p. 85. On many other points too I am in agreement with Bottéro regarding this poem and Nergal and Ereškigal.

13. See G. S. Kirk, *Myth* 110.

14. E. Reiner and Hans G. Güterbock, "The Great Prayer to Ishtar and Its Two Versions from Bogazköy," JCS 21 (1967, published 1969), 255-266, esp. p. 257.

2. NERGAL AND EREŠKIGAL: EPIC INTO ROMANCE

In the Descent of Ištar, Ereškigal rules the nether world. How it came to be that she shares this rule with Nergal who is to become her husband is told in the story of Nergal and Ereškigal.

The setting of both poems is the nether world and indeed its description, familiar from the beginning of the Descent of Ištar, is repeated, as we discussed, in Nergal and Ereškigal. It is repeated with one minor deviation and with the replacement of the final line by three other lines; more important than the deviation and the addition, however, is the place allotted to this description. It comes not at the beginning of the poem, but much later; it is inserted at the place, at about the one-third point, where the journey of Nergal to the nether world begins—of Nergal himself, and not some messenger.

The story of Nergal and Ereškigal begins not in the nether world but at the opposite pole of the cosmos, in heaven. Yet heaven is not named, nor is the nether world itself, only its queen Ereškigal, one of the two protagonists. Ereškigal's name which in the standard version of the Descent of Ištar was delayed until the twenty-fourth line, and which appeared only obliquely—in its Akkadian translation, Mistress of the Great Earth—in the earlier, Middle Assyrian, preamble to that poem, here appears in the first distich:

1 When the gods celebrated a banquet
2 They sent a messenger to their sister Ereškigal.

This introduction is from a version written down outside Mesopotamia, in Tell el-Amarna in Egypt, which can be dated to the Middle Babylonian period (fourteenth century B.C.). This copy (recension B) bears the marks of having been written as a scribal exercise. The library copy of the same poem, found at the Neo-Assyrian site of Sultantepe near Harrān in a copy which dates from the seventh century B.C. (recension A), is broken at the beginning, and may have had a different, more elaborate introduction. The Middle Babylonian version (B) immediately continues with the messenger's words to Ereškigal:

3 'We are not allowed to go down to you
4 'And you are not allowed to come up to us.
5 'Send someone to take your food to you.'

The messenger's words are directly followed by a line introducing the narration:

6 Ereškigal sent her attendant, Namtar.

(This is the same Namtar who also acts for Ereškigal in the Descent of Ištar.)

In the Neo-Assyrian version (A) an entire column of the tablet—one sixth of the poem—is devoted to bringing the action to this point. Rather than stating in just two lines the unbridgeable chasm that exists between the two regions—a chasm that is described in much the same words in the New Testament (Lk 16:26): "Between us and you there is a great gulf fixed so that they which would pass from hence to you cannot; neither can they pass to us, that would come from thence"—this version emphasizes the complexity of communication between heaven and nether world by a series of instructions, repeated messages, and other ceremonial. Although much of this first portion of the poem is fragmentary, it is evident that, first, Anu—the highest-ranking of the celestial gods—gives instructions to a celestial messenger, named Gaga, and imparts to him what he is to say to Ereškigal. Thereupon Gaga descends into the nether world and asks the gatekeeper for admittance. The gatekeeper "led Gaga through the first gate; he led Gaga through the second gate"; and so forth through all seven gates. We learn from this that a messenger's entrance is not encumbered by the special rites that Ištar had to undergo, even though the possibilities of repetition offered by the succession of the seven gates are here too exploited, in this poetry which thrives on parallelism and repetition, to delay the action. Once in Ereškigal's presence Gaga repeats Anu's message. As compared to the three-line message of the Middle Babylonian version B, the message in this late version A is seven lines long and is preceded by a three-line introduction.

27' He entered her spacious courtyard,
28' He knelt and kissed the ground before her,
29' Straightening up, he speaks to her standing:
30' 'Anu, your father, sent me.
31' He says: "You are not allowed to come up,
32' In your own year you do not come up to us,
33' And we are not allowed to descend,
34' In our own month we do not descend to you.[1]
35' Let your messenger come hither,
36' Let him remove the dish from the table and receive the present destined for you.
37' Whatever I give him he should hand over to you safely." '

Ereškigal then pronounces the appropriate greetings and Gaga replies suitably. Only then, about 65 lines into the poem, does Ereškigal instruct her attendant Namtar to go up to heaven for her portion of the banquet.

It is this errand of Namtar's that triggers the plot upon which the poem is based. Namtar is slighted by one of the gods in the divine assembly, who does not rise in his presence. This god is summoned before Ereškigal who—so the Middle Babylonian version tells us—wants to put him to death for his irreverence. The culprit is Nergal, the hero of the poem; *we* are told his name, but Ereškigal does not know it. Before setting out to obey the summons, Nergal is given elaborate instructions by Ea on how to circumvent Ereškigal's wrath and punishment; it is again Ea who is able to devise a stratagem, but its details are in part still obscure in spite of some new text material, recently published, which supplements the fragmentary sources.

Only at this juncture, when the hero embarks upon the descent into the nether world—at the end of column ii, that is, one third into the poem—is the description which began the Descent of Ištar introduced in the poem. The insertion of this description of the dark and silent realm of the dead into the narrative transforms the reader from a heretofore uninvolved party into a sympathetic participant who from this point on becomes involved in the fate of the hero, and for whose sake the suspense wrought by the threatening tableau interrupting the continuous narrative is created. Our curiosity about what lies ahead for the hero, whether he will follow Ea's advice, and if so, whether the safeguards will prove effective, remains in suspense while the poet delays the action by the description of the nether world, and not by some novel description but by one familiar to the reader from other poems.

The stratagem devised by Ea seems to comprise three sets of precautions. Of these only the last set is reasonably clear: Nergal is to refuse the marks of hospitality. He is not to sit on the chair proffered, nor eat the bread offered, nor drink the beer offered, nor accept water for washing his feet nor, finally, let himself be seduced by Ereškigal's beauty. Similar instructions about not accepting the food and drink offered in heaven are given by Ea to Adapa, hero of the like-named story who is summoned to heaven. Of course, as Adapa's story shows, the bread and drink of heaven would have conferred immortality on him; by refusing it he forfeited immortality, both for himself and for humankind. Thus, again by implicature only, but obvious to the reader and especially to the reader familiar with the Adapa story, the gifts of hospitality of the nether world are gifts spelling death.

The first set of Ea's instructions is for Nergal to take a present to Ereškigal, a throne he is to offer her as a gift sent by her father Anu, but which Nergal is to build himself from wood he cuts in the forest and decorate with paint to resemble gold and precious stones. The gift is to ensure his admittance into the nether world as Anu's messenger; the choice of a throne may have another desired effect: Ereškigal, in leaving her throne to occupy the new one, would thereby relinquish her status of queen.

Ea's stratagem must have included a third set of precautions, though these are not found in the preserved fragments of the poem, but inferred from subsequent events. It seems that Nergal was to assume a disguise, or at least was admonished not to reveal his name and identity—so far Ereškigal has not identified the god who slighted her; she keeps referring to him as "that god." Disguises to gain entrance to an inaccessible place or to enter a potentially dangerous domain under false pretenses appear in other stories as well. The Poor Man of Nippur disguises himself first as a wealthy lord bearing a royal message and secondly as a famous physician in order to enter the mayor's house and give him a good beating. The aforementioned Adapa disguises himself, again upon the advice of Ea, as a mourner for the two very gods who meet him at the gate of heaven so as to put Anu, who summoned him into his presence to punish him, into a good mood and to make him think Adapa is simple-minded.

We follow, in spite of the fragmentary state of preservation of the tablet, how Nergal obeys each instruction of Ea and how he is admitted safely into the presence of Ereškigal, even though the tenor of the dialogue that takes place between Ereškigal and Namtar before she orders him to admit Nergal remains obscure.

It is of course Ea's very last instruction that Nergal does not obey: he falls in love with Ereškigal, the pair embrace, enter her bedroom, and spend six days making love. Nergal, however, slips away before the seventh day dawns (Ea may have warned him not to spend seven full days in the nether world)[2] and tricks the gatekeeper into letting him leave by pretending that he is taking a message from Ereškigal to heaven—or so we may deduce with reasonable certitude from the fragmentary lines. Thus, when in the morning Ereškigal bids Namtar to bring food and drink to "Anu's messenger," he is obliged to tell her that Anu's messenger disappeared before dawn. Ereškigal is overcome by grief at the news that her lover has deserted her. Namtar comforts her by promising that he will fetch "that god" again. Ereškigal thereupon entrusts Namtar with a message that combines a plea for compassion with a threat. Ever since she was a young girl she has had no part in the games and dances of the girls—let the gods now send back the god who made love to her. If they do not, she threatens in the same terms Ištar uttered at the gate of the nether world,[3] she will let the dead go up and devour the living. Her way of accomplishing this would be to stop fulfilling her function as goddess of death:

column v 7 I will not decree death any longer, I will not issue verdicts for the great gods,
     8 The great gods who dwell within Irkalla.
     9 If you do not send that god here
    10 According to [the rites of Irkalla] and the Great Earth
    11 I will bring up the dead, they will devour the living,
    12 I will make the dead more numerous than the living.

Namtar's first journey to heaven to bring back Nergal is fruitless. Though he is admitted to the "courtyard" of Anu—no doubt the place of the divine assembly—and may examine each god in turn, he does not recognize Nergal. He returns to Ereškigal and reports that he saw a bald, squinting, and lame god sitting in the assembly; this, we assume, must have struck him as out of character. Ereškigal thereupon sends Namtar back to fetch "that god"; she obviously has seen through this further trick of Ea's, how he turned her lover into a malformed creature. Namtar goes up to heaven once again with his mistress's order and again examines one god after the other. Before he can get hold of the disfigured—or disguised—Nergal, he is distracted by the offer of water and oil to wash his body. Ea meanwhile has the opportunity to instruct Nergal on how to equip himself in order to avoid the perils of entering the nether world.[4] How Namtar finally finds Nergal is lost in a break on the tablet. After the break, we are at the instructions given to Nergal.

Nergal is to take along a chair and six other objects, but what these are is lost in the breaks; only the sevenfold instruction "Take along" tells us that there were seven. With this stratagem we rejoin the Descent of Ištar and the "rites" of the nether world. For when Nergal, descending from heaven and arriving at the gate of Ereškigal, asks the gatekeeper for admittance, he has to undergo a similar divestiture as Ištar who had to leave one piece of her apparel at each of the seven gates. He has to leave one of the seven objects he brought along at each of the seven gates, in a ceremonial which extends in principle over 21 lines, though only the first three-line exchange at the first gate is described in full, and for the other six only a ditto mark indicates that the exchange is to be repeated:

column vi 19   When he arrived at the gate of Ereškigal,
             20   'Gatekeeper, open the gate for me!'
             21   The gatekeeper hung [his chair in] the gate, did not let him take *[it with him]*.
             22   When *he arrived* at the second gate,[5] ditto.
             23   [When he arrived at the] third [gate], ditto.

and so forth through the seventh until he arrives at Ereškigal's "spacious courtyard."

We don't know what the objects are that Nergal—and perhaps also other visitors—had to leave at each gate. Since the first is a chair—or a throne, the same word applies—it is not likely that the remaining items are pieces of apparel like those Ištar had to take off. Nor do we know what is meant by "hanging" these items in the gate. The chair brings to mind funerary furnishings; any further guesses are likely to be proved wrong when the missing piece of the puzzle is discovered.

As Nergal enters Ereškigal's "spacious courtyard" he promptly pulls her from her throne. We expect, according to the similar turn of events described in the Middle Babylonian version B, that Ereškigal now pleads for her life, offering to share with Nergal the rule of the nether world. Not so in this later version: Nergal pulls her from the throne here too, but it is to embrace her—and there a fairy tale would add that they lived happily ever after. The Babylonian poem takes them only through six days of lovemaking, described in the same terms as when Nergal first visited Ereškigal. When the seventh day arrives—the text here has a ruling, possibly signaling some omission or repetition—Anu seems to have agreed to Nergal's remaining in the nether world; with seven days elapsed, he may—or must—stay.[6] The end of the poem is missing, and the few ends of lines are inconclusive. Nor can it be recaptured from the end of the Middle Babylonian version, for it ends—without any indication whether it is the end of the poem—with Nergal's acquiescing to Ereškigal's plea, kissing her, wiping away her tears, and uttering the rather obscure words: "what (or: whatever) you have asked of me since long-past months until now." No matter; the etiological story has been told. Other poems—hymns and prayers to Nergal—often mention his role as ruler of the nether world. Both the older and the more recent version of Nergal and Ereškigal tell how this came about in nearly identical terms, and with nearly identical episodes. Yet there is a difference between the two in that the peripeties required to make Nergal king of the nether world are kept to a minimum in the older version and are multiplied in the later one. This can be seen from the juxtaposition of the trips from heaven to the nether world and back in each version.

A Neo-Assyrian version	B Middle Babylonian version
1. Gaga, messenger from heaven to Ereškigal	1. Messenger from heaven to Ereškigal
2. Namtar, messenger from Ereškigal to heaven	2. Namtar, messenger from Ereškigal to heaven
3. [Namtar reports back to Ereškigal]	3. [Namtar reports back to Ereškigal]
4. [Ereškigal sends Namtar to heaven to summon Nergal]	4. Ereškigal sends Namtar to heaven to summon Nergal
5. Nergal descends incognito; Nergal and Ereškigal fall in love.	5. ------------------
6. Nergal slips away and goes back to heaven	6. ------------------
7. Ereškigal sends Namtar to heaven to look for Nergal	7. ------------------
8. Namtar returns reporting that he did not find Nergal	8. Namtar returns reporting that he did not find Nergal

9. Ereškigal sends Namtar back to heaven for Nergal	9. **
10. a) Nergal goes down to the nether world	10. a) Nergal goes down to the nether world
10. b) and stays there for love of Ereškigal	10. b) and forces Ereškigal into submission

The earlier version (B), as this comparison shows, lacks the episode in which Nergal, instead of appearing as a culprit summoned before Ereškigal, arrives in the nether world incognito and under false pretenses and seduces Ereškigal. This plot necessitates not only a trip back and forth by Nergal—with the accompanying trappings—but also two trips of Namtar to heaven and back. Namtar's trips now have the object of bringing to the nether world not the arrogant god who had slighted Ereškigal's messenger but Ereškigal's lover.

The role of Namtar differs in the two versions in other ways too. In the earlier recension (B), when the gatekeeper announces to Namtar that "a god"—Nergal summoned—waits at the gate, Namtar recognizes in him the god who would not rise to greet him. He reports this to Ereškigal who bids him to let in the god so that she may kill him. Namtar thereupon greets Nergal with great courtesy, pretending not to have recognized him. In the later version (A) it is to Ereškigal that the gatekeeper announces the arrival of the visitor—Nergal posing as messenger from Anu—and asks that his credentials be examined, literally, that someone identify him. The task of identification devolves upon Namtar. It appears that in this version too Namtar recognizes the god waiting at the gate, but a break on the tablet prevents us from learning whether he dissembles this fact or not. We are told, instead, that Namtar is seized by terror or rage, an emotion described with the same words as Ereškigal's reaction in the Descent of Ištar upon hearing of Ištar's seeking admittance:

> 'His face became pale like a cut-off tamarisk,
> His lips turned black like a *kunīnu* plant."

Ereškigal, before asking him to let "the god" enter, warns Namtar not to aspire to the highest divine rank (which we had not been told he was seeking) and proposes that he take her place on the throne and hand down the judgments of the nether world while she herself goes up to heaven to eat and drink with her father Anu.

**The fragmentary state of the text makes it impossible to tell whether this trip occurred in the Middle Babylonian version or not. If it did, there was room only for Ereškigal's instructions, not for the description of Namtar's trip.

Nergal's repeated descents in the late version call forth the elaborate charades that Ea has devised. In the earlier version Ea merely gives Nergal a retinue of fourteen demons to station at the fourteen (not seven) gates of the nether world. The role these demons play is not too clear since Nergal's words, "Let the gates be opened *or else* I will run *with/for* you," spoken to them or possibly to Namtar, are still obscure.[7] They seem, however, to provide the military force needed to enter. In the late version, on the other hand, Ea's instructions to Nergal involve fashioning and taking along various objects: on his first descent a throne as a gift to Ereškigal and on the second seven objects so that Nergal has something to leave with the nether world's gatekeeper whose duty, it appears, is to divest visitors at each of the seven gates.

This divestiture obtains, however, only on Nergal's second descent when he journeys down under his own name. Messengers—Gaga, Namtar, and Nergal himself on his first entrance when he pretends to be Anu's messenger—seem to come and go without further ado. We are reminded of Aṣûšu-namir, the messenger sent by Ea in the Descent of Ištar to obtain Ištar's release, who also was directly admitted into the nether world while Ištar was forced to leave a piece of attire at each gate. Messengers, thus, seem to have the privilege—the diplomatic immunity—to move about freely between the various realms, whereas the gods themselves cannot cross the boundaries of their assigned domains without incurring the risks associated with such transgressions. Were it not, precisely, for the beginning of the story of Nergal and Ereškigal where this interdiction is expressly stated, we would have to infer it solely from the episodes related in the stories set in the nether world.

Not even Nergal descends of his own accord; it is only Ištar who "set her mind" on the descent to the nether world—for reasons that are not given in the story. Nor does Babylonian literature tell of any human, be he hero or demigod, who makes the journey and returns unharmed, as did Theseus rescued by Heracles or, later, Aeneas, and in his wake Dante. Only in a dream can a human visit the nether world, as is told in the story about an Assyrian crown prince's Vision of the Nether World.[8] Even Gilgameš, part divine but part human, who, not having found the eternal life he was seeking, became, it is true, the judge of the nether world, did not return from there. His return is not from the nether world but from the end of the world where his quest of immortality had taken him to seek out the survivor from the Flood who dwells there immortal. This quest, therefore, is not a *Descensus*—though it is fraught with similar dangers, such as crossing the "waters of death"—but more properly belongs in the tradition of other journeys to the end of the world, such as the one related in the Alexander romances. In the course of the journey to fabulous lands Alexander the Great, like Gilgameš, passes through a jeweled garden, and encounters an even greater variety of strange creatures than the scorpion-men who, in the Gilgameš Epic, guard the entrance to the mountain through which the sun passes during the night hours and through which Gilgameš himself has to pass.

The additional episodes that the story of Nergal and Ereškigal acquired in the course of its elaboration affect not only the lesser characters but, most of all, the protagonists. Ereškigal becomes the heroine of a love story, though whether in the role of the seduced and abandoned woman or of the woman scorned is not quite clear; perhaps the story unites both topoi. Her character and behavior were perplexing already in the Descent of Ištar, where too we encountered her more often distraught than queenly. But in Nergal and Ereškigal she is not lacking in shrewdness: she will not be taken in by Ea's ruse as she was in the Descent of Ištar. She realizes that the disfigured god whom Namtar saw in heaven was none other than the god who, in the earlier version, slighted her messenger and, in the later version, abandoned her. These traits may warrant an alternative interpretation. Only in the early version does Ereškigal state that she wants to kill the irreverent god. The corresponding section is missing in the late recension, but her words and actions seem to imply a different goal. The strange tirade she addresses to Namtar when he reports to her that "Anu's messenger" is the god who had slighted him—a section only recently recovered:

> O Namtar, do not seek the highest divine rank
> And do not set your heart on heroic deeds.
> Go and sit on the royal throne
> And hand down the judgments of the nether world.
> I will go up to the heaven of my father Anu,
> Eat the food of my father Anu,
> Drink the beer of my father Anu   (W iii 5'-10')

could mean that she is ready to use the visit of one of the *di superi* to seduce him and thus to achieve her aim of ascending to heaven. After the careful appropriate preparations of taking a bath—a motif well known from the Sumerian myth of 'Enlil and Ninlil,' and discussed by Kirk, p. 99 and 101f.—she succeeds in seducing the god, but he leaves her. She cannot keep him in the nether world because he has refused, upon Ea's advice, the tokens of hospitality, and she has no power over him because he has withheld his name from her. In her lament over his desertion she refers to him by the name Erra (another name for the god of the nether world (originally two different gods, Erra and Nergal became syncretized at some point in history). Unless one assumes[9] that by her words: "Erra, the lover who gave me pleasure, I was not sated with the pleasure he gave me, he has left me" Ereškigal means that her previous husband, Erra, did not satisfy her and she longs for the god whose name is not known to her, we must conclude that Nergal, when he slept with Ereškigal, pretended to be Erra. This again is a well-known folktale motif and may have had a piquant reference—as Odysseus' giving his name as Oûtis, "Nobody," to Polyphemus—which eludes us since we have no sure etymology, in Sumerian or Akkadian, for the name Erra.

In order to regain her lover, Ereškigal has to resort to a tearful plea to the heavenly gods, though her plea is made urgent by a threat. Her appeal for the return of her lover may be, if the alternative interpretation is correct, but a ploy of the woman scorned seeking revenge. Thus, when Nergal eventually returns to Ereškigal, his renewed lovemaking with her and his staying in the nether world—and here we rejoin the earlier version—is possibly as much the result of coercion as it was when Nergal pulled her from the throne. The woman scorned—or the woman abandoned—has had her revenge, or her satisfaction, or both, but at the price of sharing her power with Nergal in the nether world.

NOTES

1. The parallelism of "in your own year" and "in our own month," that is, the use of two words from one semantic field (here the calendar) but of different meaning, is not usual in Babylonian poetry, where the two parallel words have to be synonymous, but it is a common device in Ugaritic poetry. Note that recension B omits "in your (own) year" and "in our (own) month."

2. This was suggested by R. Labat, in idem, A. Cacquot, M. Sznycer, and M. Vieyra, *Les religions du Proche-Orient asiatique* (Paris, 1970), pp. 107f.

3. The same threat is uttered by Ištar not only when she descends to the nether world but also in order to obtain from Anu the bull whom she wants to send against Gilgameš to punish him for having jilted her.

4. The present state of the text seems to put the instructions into Namtar's mouth, but the role of cunning trickster would better fit Ea. A more complete version of the text, when found, may decide this point of the story.

5. Or "the second gatekeeper."

6. In the Rabbinical tradition, an "angel" (literally, "messenger," like *angelos*) sent down from heaven on a mission may not stay on earth seven days in a row; if he does, he cannot return to heaven. References from Yalqut Khadash fol. 117 col. 3 no. 53 and from Menahem Recanati are quoted in J. A. Eisenmenger, *Entdecktes Judenthum* (Königsberg, 1711) vol. II 387, to which a note in R. H. Charles, *The Book of Enoch* (Oxford 1893) p. 64, note to VI 6, drew my attention.

7. Bottéro interprets these instructions as given to Namtar "and his personnel" after Nergal had his demons secure the entrances to the center where Ereškigal dwells. However, in the Vision of the Nether World (see note 8), fourteen netherworld demons guard the gates of the nether world.

8. Published by W. von Soden, "Die Unterweltsvision eines assyrischen Kronprinzen," ZA 43 (1936), 1-31; see also idem, WO 7 (1973/4), p. 237, where the political background of the story is expounded. For the history and significance of the motif see Elisabeth Frenzel, *Motive der Weltliteratur*, 2nd ed., Stuttgart: Kröner 1980, sub Unterweltsbesuch.

9. D. O. Edzard, *Wörterbuch der Mythologie* I 110: Mesopotamien—Nergal und Ereškigal. His interpretation is also doubted by E. von Weiher, *Der babylonische Gott Nergal* (AOAT 11), p. 51 n. 2.

Two lion-griffins attacking bull between them.
Middle Assyrian cylinder seal (14th cent. B.C.)
in the Pierpont Morgan Library Collection, New York.

Chapter III

THE NEWS OF VICTORY

There are no Babylonian poems which describe wars among gods, no Titanomachia comparable to the Greek. Instead of pitched battles between opposing camps, there are only jousts between two individuals: a champion, representing the gods, and an adversary. They are comparable to the confrontations between two such representatives of opposing parties as Hector and Achilles, an oracle for the ensuing battle; or David and Goliath, a substitute for battle.

The two jousts that form the core of two Babylonian epic poems are fought for the retrieval of the "Tablet of Destinies." This tablet, held in the god's hand or worn on his chest, gives him the power to command the universe.[1] Twice in poems narrating the exploits of gods this tablet falls into the wrong hands, and the gods must send out a champion to retrieve it.

As long as the tablet is in their possession, the supreme triad of gods who divided among themselves the universe—heaven, subterranean waters, and the region between the two, including the earth and its inhabitants—need do no more than pronounce an order to annihilate the forces that dare rise against them. They do not engage in battle; when the divine powers are prevented from operating, it is one of the next generation of gods, a youthful warrior god, who goes into action. One such youthful champion is Marduk, another is Ninurta. Their exploits are related in the Poem of Creation and in the Story of Anzû. In addition to other topics each of these poems contains the description of single combat between the divine champion and the unlawful possessor of the Tablet of Destinies.

While descriptions of hand-to-hand combats are rare, there are iconographic attestations that they existed. The representations of two grappling heroes that are known from seals and reliefs[2] do not allow us to determine whether the encounter takes place in a battle or in some wrestling match. One such famous wrestling match between Gilgameš and Enkidu is described in the Epic of Gilgameš (Tablet P, vi 16ff.; see CAD s.v. *lâdu*) and has been identified as belt-wrestling by A. L. Oppenheim (Orientalia NS 17 [1948] 29f.). The making of representations of wrestling twins, painted or in the round, for apotropaic purposes is described in rituals,[3] though their function in the ritual is not further specified.

61

In single combat the individual represents, and fights for, a collectivity; in the two Babylonian poems, it is the entire assembly of the gods that is threatened, by Tiamat in the Poem of Creation, by Anzû in the Story of Anzû. The divine champion affronts a being who is not anthropomorphic as the gods are: Marduk Tiamat, the primeval sea, and Ninurta Anzû, a bat-like winged creature[4] who is represented as a giant bird sometimes with a lion's head and sometimes with a bat's head, but in the myth that deals with his defeat is essentially featureless.[5]

To persuade the god to do battle with the monster and wrest from it the Tablet of Destinies, the assembly of the gods has to promise supreme rank to their chosen champion. The poems that deal with these jousts therefore serve as etiological stories of the rise of a young god. The Poem of Creation exalts Marduk to supremacy over the gods; in the Story of Anzû, whose hero, Ninurta, was never raised to such supreme rank, it is Ninurta's mother, Mami—the mother goddess in several stories about the gods—who is promised the rank of Mistress of All Gods if she sends out her son against Anzû.[6]

The assembled gods not only cajole and promise but are also committed to suitably equipping their champion. In addition, in the Poem of Creation they subject Marduk to a test to make sure that he too, by his word alone, is able "to destroy and to create."

> They placed in their midst a *lumāšu* star;
> they spoke to their offspring Marduk:
> "O Lord, your decree shall be equal to that of the other gods;
> to destroy and to create—say but the word and let these be done.
> At your word let the *lumāšu* star be destroyed,
> speak to it again and let the *lumāšu* be re-established."
> He spoke and at his word the *lumāšu* star was destroyed;
> he spoke to it again, and the *lumāšu* star was re-created.
>   (Poem of Creation IV 19-26)

Thereupon they proclaim him king; bestow on him the insignia of kingship: scepter, throne, and *palû* (mantle?); and give him an irresistible weapon. Only then do they tell him, "Go and cut the throat of Tiamat."

Although Marduk in return undertakes to defeat not only Tiamat but also the eleven monstrous creatures she has created and at whose head she has placed, as general, her husband Kingu, the scene which deals with their defeat involves only Marduk and Tiamat. Four times are we told, first in the narrative, and then in reports from or instructions to messengers who repeat verbatim these actions of Tiamat, how she created fearsome monsters and made their fangs drip poison, how she singled out Kingu to lead this cohort, and how she exalted his power by placing the Tablet of Destinies on his chest—though how she came to possess it herself is not told. Yet Marduk challenges only Tiamat. A verbal challenge, as both this and the Anzû episode show, was therefore a required preliminary to single combat.

Tiamat, who had planned to repulse Marduk with a magic word (called *tû*; most commonly designating an incantatory formula), upon being so challenged accepts a hand-to-hand combat. Marduk had equipped himself for this combat. In addition to the "irresistible weapon" received from the gods he fitted himself out with a weapon called Deluge, fashioned a bow and arrows and a net, created seven evil winds in addition to the four winds that his father Anu had given him as playthings when a child, and harnessed four storms to his chariot. But he also arms himself with the magic word and takes along an herb that is an antidote for poison (whether against the poisonous fangs of the monsters or against some poison spewed forth by Tiamat herself is not said). The magic word is an appropriate weapon for Marduk who, like Ea, is the exorcist god par excellence and the patron god of the exorcist. Ea himself had used this *tû* to put Apsû to sleep (I 62), and Marduk is sent out by Anšar to "calm" *(šupšuhu)* Tiamat with his pure *tû* in an earlier reference to the upcoming battle (II 117).

Of these elaborate trappings he needs only the net. When Tiamat approaches in answer to Marduk's challenge ("Even though the mass of your army is ready, even though they have girt the weapons you gave them, let you and me confront each other, let us do battle"), he spreads the net and ensnares her. This net *(saparru)* must be like the one depicted on the Stele of Vultures and other reliefs[7] which show the victor holding his enemies enmeshed in a net. He then lets loose the evil winds, and Tiamat, falling into the trap, opens her mouth to swallow them. When her belly is bloated with the winds, Marduk pierces it with his arrow so that she bursts. At the sight of Marduk killing Tiamat her army flees in disarray. Marduk ensnares them too in his net, breaks their weapons, and puts the monsters in chains. No battle between armies has ensued whatsoever, and not even the promised clash of weapons between Marduk and Tiamat has taken place. Tiamat has been outwitted. Marduk takes back the Tablet of Destinies from Kingu and places it on his own chest where he will wear it as an insigne of his kingship over the gods.

The episode of Ninurta's encounter with Anzû happens under quite different circumstances, yet can be seen to conform to the same pattern, with many similarities even in the details. Anzû, who had snatched the Tablet of Destinies from Enlil in an unguarded moment, has fled with it to the mountains, alone. He has no army, no retinue; any confrontation with him will obviously be individual. Ninurta, upon the advice and with the help of his mother, is also armed with bow and arrows—poisoned arrows, to boot; he carries the poison, not, like Marduk, an antidote to the enemy's poison. He too has seven evil winds at his disposal; they serve as winged steeds for his chariot. The winds which accompanied Marduk were intended to throw waves, for Tiamat is the sea: the text says "to disturb the bosom of Tiamat." In the mountains where Ninurta pursues Anzû the winds throw up a cloud of dust and thus veil the features of the approaching god, in a tactic his mother had directed Ninurta to use.

When Anzû sees Ninurta advancing upon him he is seized with rage, just as Tiamat was after Marduk challenged her. But Anzû cannot see Ninurta. His first words, as at the meeting of two visored knights, are a demand for identification: "Who are you who come against me? Reveal yourself! *(ṭēmka idna)*" And Ninurta answers, "I have come, the one who will trample you"—without identifying himself. The ensuing combat is not described; all that is said is that the arms clash and the sun itself is obscured. We expect the coup de grâce to come from Ninurta's poisoned arrow. He shoots it off toward Anzû—and here it is that the power of the magic word effectively intervenes. Tiamat's magic word *(tû)*—whose nature we never learned—was of no avail, and Marduk was able to ensnare her. In Ninurta's encounter with Anzû we are told what his magic words are, but they are not qualified as *tû*. Anzû calls out to the arrow, stops it in its flight, and renders it ineffective by depriving bow and arrow of their functional form and reducing them to mere reed, wood, and tendon, properly belonging to the canebrake, the woods, and the sheep.[8]

> "Arrow, you who have come here, return to your canebrake,
> Frame of the bow, to your forests,
> String, return to the sheep's leg, feathers, to the birds."

As long as Anzû, by his words alone, can turn the assemblage of material objects that function as tools back into their mere material components, Ninurta will be powerless. He will have to resort, as so many heroes do, to the cunning of Ea. He tells Adad—the storm god, who finds himself there we know not how—to report his predicament to Ea. Adad, acting as messenger, repeats Ninurta's words to Ea, including a verbatim repetition of Anzû's magic words. Ea realizes that it is the faculty of speech that makes Anzû invulnerable. Therefore Anzû has to be deprived of this faculty with which, just as other divine or demonic beings, he is endowed and, bird that he is, be reduced to uttering only a birdcall. Ea explains to Adad the stratagem that Ninurta is to follow, and Adad brings the message back to Ninurta.

First, Ninurta should clip the wings of Anzû. At the sight of his clipped wings, Anzû will cry *kappī kappī* "My wing, my wing!," and thereafter Ninurta need fear him no more. Ninurta follows the advice— how he accomplishes the tricky business of clipping Anzû's wings we are not told, though apparently he manages without difficulty. At the sight of his clipped wings, Anzû calls out *kappī kappī* and can no longer conjure the bow and arrow. This *kappī kappī* is a known birdcall and is so listed in a poem which describes birds and their calls, interpreting them as intelligible words and sentences.[9] But this call also alludes to one of Ištar's unfortunate lovers, the *alallu* bird, whose wings Ištar broke so that now he sits in the forest and cries *kappī* (Epic of Gilgameš Tablet VI).

The victorious Ninurta ascends to the highest region of heaven and terrifies the gods with his splendor. He is given due praise and, presumably, the promised worship, and his mother the promised title "Mistress of All Gods." This whole final part of the story is preserved only on some fragmentary tablets and cannot be adequately reconstructed.

Yet not only the defeat of the enemy is important, but also making this defeat known to the concerned world. Therefore, after Ea has instructed Ninurta in how to deprive Anzû of speech, he also tells him to shoot an arrow at Anzû so that the feathers fly around, and to have the winds carry the feathers as tidings to Enlil.

This motif is not known from Sumerian epics but is repeatedly expressed in Akkadian contexts. There has to be tangible proof of having killed or reduced to helplessness the adversary. In the Poem of Creation this tangible proof is the blood of Tiamat: "[Marduk] slit open the veins carrying her blood and had the north wind carry (the blood) as tidings.[10] When his fathers saw this, they rejoiced and celebrated, they had presents taken to him in greeting" (IV 131ff.). In the Story of Anzû the winds carry Anzû's feathers as tidings to Ekur, where Ninurta's father Enlil waits to hear the outcome of the joust. Though the account of this event is not preserved, the motif appears in each set of instructions and its repetitions by the messengers. The first occurrence is in Tablet II 18-19, in the exhortation given to Ninurta by his mother: "(Capture Anzû) let the winds bring his wings as tidings to Ekur, to your father Enlil." The same lines are repeated in II 114-115, as part of Ea's instructions given to the messenger Adad, and again in II 136-137, as Adad repeats Ea's words to Ninurta. Since the part of the poem dealing with the actual defeat of Anzû is not preserved, the final account of how the winds carried Anzû's wings to Enlil is lost. That this had taken place we infer from a passage toward the end of Tablet III (CT 46 42 ii 9-12), in which another messenger speaks to Ninurta: "Your father Enlil has sent me [. . .] saying: 'The gods have heard that [you defeated] evil Anzû in the midst of the mountains. They rejoiced and celebrated and [. . .]'" (This messenger is a little-known god, Birdu, who does not otherwise appear in the preserved parts of the Story of Anzû).

The tidings of the defeat awaited by the assembly of the gods are brought by the winds, not by messengers like the famous messengers who brought the news of the defeat of the Persians at Marathon or, in Aeschylus' *Agamemnon,* of the defeat of Troy. Winds also play other roles, as we have seen: they accompany the hero in battle, draw his chariot, obscure his appearance, or even help to bring about the enemy's defeat, as when they distend the belly of Tiamat. The herald wind in the Poem of Creation is specifically the north wind, elsewhere characterized as "the propitious breath of the lord of the gods." It is propitious because as "the shearer of the sky," that is, the wind that sweeps away the clouds, it brings cool air from the mountains, as opposed to the south wind which brings the hot air and dust storms from the Gulf. Only Esarhaddon calls the south wind too the "sweet breath of Ea" and sees in it the wind that forebodes good for kingship.[11]

The role of messengers in Babylonian epics is usually restricted, as in the Poem of Creation and the Story of Anzû, to carrying reports to some deity and bringing back instructions. The messengers are always divine, that is, they belong to the story's cast of characters. These divine messengers act like their human counterparts who carry letters—written reports or instructions—to a distant correspondent. Yet even human messengers carry tangible tokens, as do the winds in the epic texts. Tangible tokens are required as proof of the veracity of ecstatics and prophets, as we have recently learned from the Mari texts. The person who reports the prophecy sends along with his report a lock of the hair and the fringe of the garment of the ecstatic. If we compare this practice to first-millennium queries for oracles (submitted to Šamaš and Adad to be answered through signs and features in the exta of the lamb to be slaughtered), in which the person who makes the request for the divinatory answer or on whose behalf the request is made is designated as "the owner of the nailmark and the fringe,' we may assume that the ecstatic's hair and fringe were submitted to verification by extispicy—a procedure also followed in the event of celestial omens under Nabonidus (Chapter I Part 1). But more pertinent to the winds' role are the tangible tokens of victory—even if not always identifiable—that the Neo-Assyrian kings had carried by messengers. In an episode about the campaigns of Sargon, the victorious general sends such tokens to the king encamped elsewhere: "His messenger, who carried the good news, brought to me in the city of Sama'una one thousand of (the enemies') *zīm pani*"—an as yet unidentified part of the soldiers' equipment or body.[12] And the legend on a relief from Assurbanipal's palace,[13] which shows soldiers in a chariot holding aloft the head of the defeated Elamite king Teumman, describes the scene as follows: "This is the head of Teumman, king of Elam, which a common soldier from my army cut off in the heat of battle; they are bringing it to Assyria as good news post haste."

NOTES

1. See Jean Bottéro, Ecole Pratique des Hautes Etudes, IVe section, sciences historiques et philologiques, Annuaire 1970/1971, pp. 122f. The famous Assyrian

King List also seems to have been worn by the king on his chest to symbolize his authority.

2. This is the interpretation given by Walter Burkert to the relief from Tell Halaf representing two grappling figures. See Winfried Orthmann, *Untersuchungen zur späthethitischen Kunst,* Bonn: Rudolf Habelt, 1971, pl. 10c (= Tell Halaf A3/49); cf. ibid. p. 403 (also in Max Freiherr von Oppenheim, *Der Tell Halaf,* Leipzig: Brockhaus, 1931, pl. 56b, opposite p. 161).

3. Examples are AAA 22 90:172f.; AfO 14 150:215ff.

4. For Anzû, see Benno Landsberger, WZKM 57 (1961) 1ff., especially pp. 9f.

5. For an analogy drawn between the two poems see also W. G. Lambert, ZDMG, Supplement III,1 (1977) pp. 70f.

6. See William L. Moran, JCS 31 (1979) 68f.

7. The Stele of Vultures is described by Donald P. Hansen, in *Propyläen-Kunstgeschichte,* vol. 14 (Berlin, 1975), p. 189 and No. 90 (photo); for another relief with net see Pierre Amiet, ibid. p. 195, ad no. 100. Amiet published another similar stela fragment in RA 66 (1972) 108, fig. 12 (a reference for which I am indebted to my colleague McGuire Gibson).

8. The bow of Aqhat is made of the same components in the Ugaritic myth of the same name, see lastly W. G. E. Watson, "The Composite Bow," *Ugarit-Forschungen* 8 (1976) 372f.

9. See W. G. Lambert, "The Birdcall Text," *Anatolian Studies* 20 (1970), 111-117.

10. This is the translation of the word written *b/pu-su-ra-tim* in CAD B 346f. (1965), but the word is still interpreted as *puz(u)rāti,* 'secret (places),' in von Soden, AHw. 885b. The meaning 'tidings' and not 'secret (places), is confirmed by the use of the verb *b/pussuru* 'to bring tidings' (which belongs to the same root as *bussurātum*) in a Neo-Assyrian cultic text in which Anzû's defeat is mentioned: Anzû kašid ... alik ana ilāni gabbu passir upassaršunu ('he said in front of Anšar) "Anzû has been defeated" (and Anšar said to him) "Go, take the news to all the gods," and he took the news to them.' W. von Soden, ZA 51 (1955) 138:59f. and parallel ibid. 154 r. 6.

11. Borger Esarhaddon p. 45 ii 3.

12. Lie Sargon 451.

13. Streck Assurbanipal p. 312, epigraph.

Chapter IV

A HYMN TO THE SUN

In the literature of many nations, hymns to the sun have achieved special fame. From Egypt, we have the hymn of Akhnaton to the Sun;[1] from Rome, an anonymous poem (Anthologia Latina I no. 389); medieval hymns address Jesus as Sol salutis, Sol justitiae, Sol sine solstitio[2] (the famed Canticle to Brother Sun of Saint Francis of Assisi, notwithstanding its title, addresses the sun only in its first verses). Similarly, among Babylonian poems the hymn to the Sun god Šamaš occupies a special place. It is one of the few well-preserved hymns that belong to the group of 200-line poems. The same number of verses, 200, also make up Poem IV of Prudentius's Peristephanon; they break down into 50 sapphic strophes "thus too long for performance," suggests Charles Witke.[3] The Babylonian hymn's 200 lines are divided into 100 distichs, again too long for oral performance as individual prayer, or even for recitation at some solemn occasion; at least, there is no indication that it was so used. One hundred lines were considered the optimal length of a poem by Edgar Allan Poe as he decided, as first consideration upon embarking on writing "The Raven," the dimensions of the poem yet to be written, even though his essay about it, "The Philosophy of Composition," seems to be a later rationalization.

The sun for the Babylonians is, first of all, the celestial body that gives light and warmth. It rises, as the cylinder seals depict it, between two mountains in the east and dissipates the darkness. In the course of the year, as it returns to the Vernal equinox point, it regulates not only the seasons, but also the civil calendar, which had to be adjusted by intercalary months (the "leap-year" system of the Babylonians) whenever the annual cycle of the twelve lunar months had fallen behind the solar year.

The sun is also the god from whom nothing is hidden. For this reason, no doubt, he is the god of justice. By his authority laws are promulgated, and remissions of debts decreed. The greatest praise given to a king is that he is "the sun of his people" *(šamaš nišēšu)*, an epithet going back to King Hammurapi. For the same reason the sun is also the patron god of the diviner: it is the sun god who inscribes the future in the entrails of the sheep for the haruspex to read when he examines the liver and lungs of the sacrificial animal.

The Šamaš hymn treats all these aspects of the sun god. Its central part focuses on Šamaš's role as god of justice. Its message is that justice and fairness are pleasing to Šamaš, while dishonesty is abhorrent to him. Instead of dealing with this aspect of Šamaš in abstract terms, the poet illustrates his point by enumerating people from all walks of life; in each group the just act in a way pleasing to Šamaš, and the wicked earn Šamaš's displeasure and are punished by him. This enumeration takes the form of antithetic distichs—a device that testifies to the artistic sophistication of the poet.

The poem's ethical message is enclosed by a frame in which the god is depicted as the luminary par excellence. At the beginning of the poem, he is described with reference to his daily course, from sunrise to nightfall, and his nocturnal journey underground to return to the sunrise point. At the end of the poem, incompletely preserved, the poet returns to the luminary and describes him as the regulator of the calendar and the seasons. The transitions from the sun's daily course to the moral message, and from it, again, to his yearly course are achieved through references to the sun's omniscience; and these lead naturally to his role as the patron of divination.

Thus, undeniably, the poem has a definite structure, even if it occasionally contains some verses that do not bear on the topic of a particular section and seem mere fillers, repeating some of the more common attributes of Šamaš. Such fillers may have been added to stretch the hymn to its predetermined length of two hundred verses. No such fillers appear in the central part. It is therefore likely that the poem was conceived around this central part, as a praise to the sun as the heavenly body which brings the light of day and regulates the seasons, but especially as the all-seeing god who discerns between the just and the wicked. When these topics fell short of two hundred lines, some lines were added wherever a transition or some association made it feasible.

A horizontal ruling after every second line on the tablet makes the poem appear to consist of one hundred distichs. In reality, the rulings are purely mechanical. Besides couplets, admittedly the most frequent, there are also groups of three lines, as will become apparent. Nor is it possible to divide these two hundred lines into twenty ten-line stanzas, such as appear to be the units of other examples of hymnal poetry. Rather, as I shall attempt to show, the poem is structured in six parts of unequal length. As befits a long poem, its parts are themselves long; only short poems contain short strophes. I shall examine these six parts, one by one.

The first part consists of 24 lines:

Part I

Illuminator of the entirety of heavens,
    Brightener of darkness for mankind far and wide,

>   O Sun, illuminator of the entirety of heavens,
>   Brightener of darkness for mankind far and wide,
> 5   Your rays, like a net, are cast over the earth;
>   Of the remotest mountains you lighten the shadows.
>   At your appearance the nether world gods and chthonic gods rejoiced;
>   All the Igigu-gods greet you with joy.
>   Constantly your rays are penetrating into hidden places,
> 10   By your bright light men's steps are revealed.
>   Your sheen seeks out [. . .]
>   You [set aglow], like fire, the ends of the world.
>   You open wide the gates of all [sanctuaries],
>   From all the Igigu you [receive] offerings.
> 15   O Sun, as you rise, men are on their knees,
>   [. . .] all lands.
>   Illuminator of darkness, opener of the udders of heaven,
>   Hastener of dawn's [. . .] to the grain-fields that sustain the land.
>   The remotest mountains are overlaid with your brilliance,
> 20   Your radiance fills the expanse of all lands.
>   Bending over the mountains, you oversee the earth,
>   You hold the world disk suspended from the middle of the sky.
>   You care for all peoples of all lands,
>   All those King Ea has created are entrusted into your care.

The somewhat stilted phrases "Illuminator . . . of heavens," "Brightener of darkness," which appear in the first four lines, and "Illuminator of darkness," "Opener of the udders of heaven," "Hastener of dawn," which cluster in lines 17-18, have been deliberately chosen to render the constructions of the original, namely participial constructions. Participles do not specify either tense or person as would constructions with finite verbs, such as "You are the illuminator of heavens" or "You illuminate the heavens." The Akkadian constructions correspond rather closely to the compounds so frequent in medieval Latin hymns, such as *rerum conditor, noctis . . . pervigil*. In these lines, the poet chose the participle instead of some other verbal construction equally available in the language.

For a translation to be as faithful to the text as possible it should render the grammatical constructions of the original with precise equivalents if comparable constructions are available. In this particular poem, as we shall see, the variety of the syntactical constructions and their interplay constitute a compositional device. Therefore I have chosen to render the Akkadian participles with English nouns. By following the poet's choices we are better able to follow the articulation of the poem.

The participles that I have translated by nouns cluster in the first twenty-odd lines of the poem; the first two of the five cited occur twice each, making a total of seven occurrences in the first eighteen lines. In these same twenty-odd lines finite verb forms are conspicuously absent; instead of verbs conjugated for tense, a nominal construction peculiar to Akkadian is used throughout, the so-called "stative" or predicative adjective, which is here translated as "are . . . ," "are . . .-ing." Note "Your rays, like a net, are cast over the earth" (line 5); "Constantly your rays are penetrating into hidden places" (line 9); "O Sun, as you rise, men are on their knees" (15); "The remotest mountains are overlaid with your brilliance" (19). By contrast, in the first twenty-four lines only six finite verbs refer to the sun: "Of the remotest mountains you lighten the shadows" (6), "Your sheen seeks out [. . .]" (11), "You open wide the gates of all [sanctuaries]" (13), "Your radiance fills the expanse of all lands" (20), "Bending over the mountains, you oversee the earth" (21), and "You care for all peoples of all lands" (25); moreover, three of these, in lines 20, 21, and 23, that is, toward the end of Part I, alternate with the just-mentioned nominal construction used in "you *hold* the world disk *suspended* from the middle of the sky" in line 22, and "All those King Ea has created *are entrusted* into your care" in line 24 or even occur side by side with it as "you oversee" does with "Bending over" in one and the same line 21. Two other finite verbs in lines 7 and 8 depict the joy of the gods at the sight of the sun: "At your appearance the (nether world) gods and chthonic gods rejoiced; All the Igigu-gods greet you with joy." In all, there are eight verbs, as opposed to 14 nominal forms: seven participles and seven predicative adjectives.

Nowhere else in the poem do we find this peculiar distribution of predicates. This in itself sets these first twenty-four lines apart; with their concentration of timeless participles and predicative adjectives they constitute a static tableau.

Part II goes from line 25 to line 98.

Part II

25   You shepherd all those who are endowed with breath,
       You alone are their pastor above and below.
     You keep crossing the sky faithfully,
       You pass over the wide earth every day.
     Over high seas, mountains, earth, and sky
30   Like . . . you pass faithfully every day.
     Below, in the nether world, you care for the demons, the Kubu, and
         the Anunnaki,
       Above, you lead all who dwell on earth in the right path.
     Shepherd of the regions below, pastor of the regions above,
       You, Sun, are the regulator of the light of the universe.

35 You cross and recross the wide expanse of the sea
Whose depths not even the Igigu know.
O, Sun, your blaze descends even to the underground waters,
And the creatures of the sea look upon your light.
O Sun, you tie like a cord, you cover like a fog,
40 Your broad protection is spread over all lands.
You toil every day, your face never darkens,
You bide your time through the night passing through [...].
Over unknown and faraway regions, and over countless miles
You, Sun, labor sleeplessly: what you covered by day you retrace at night.[4]
45 There is none among the Igigu who toils as hard as you,
None among all the gods of the world who is as supreme as you are.
At your rising the gods of all lands gathered,
Your fearsome sheen covers the land.
Of all countries, diversified as their tongues may be,
50 You detect the plans, you observe their ways.
On their knees before you are all men,
O Sun, the universe longs for your light.
To the diviner's bowl, to the ... of cedar
You ... the dream interpreters who explain the dreams.
55 Those who make sworn *treaties* are on their knees before you,
The wicked and the just alike are on their knees before you.
Without you, no one steps into the abyss (for the ordeal),
You are the one who brings light to the case of the evil and the criminal.
(59 broken)
60 If sleep descends upon him [...]
You make the cheater, surrounded by [...], turn back (from the ordeal),
You have rise from the river of the ordeal the [innocent] involved in a lawsuit.
Through the just verdict, O Sun, that you pronounced [...]
Your words are manifest, and cannot be changed, [...]
65 You stand by the traveler whose path is narrow,
You give succour to the seafarer who fears the waves.
You lead the hunter on unexplored roads,
He who prays to the Sun can follow the tracks.
You save from the high waters the merchant who carries his weights,
70 You rescue him who sinks to the depths, you give him wings.
You point out a harbor to (those) in the midst of the sea and the desert,
To the deported you show roads known to the sun.

You liberate him who is thrown in a hidden dungeon,
You save him who was snatched away and is in prison.
75 He whose god [...]
When he sees [...]
You stand by the sick [...]
You decide his case [...]
You bring [...]
80 From the nether world you [...]
The angry goddesses [...]
You are majestic, you do not [...]
O Sun, from your net [...]
From your traps [...]
85 He who [...] to the oath
Who does not fear [...]
Your net is stretched, [your...] is far-flung
He who coveted the wife of his partner
Will [...] before his appointed time.
90 A twisted snare is readied for him [...]
Your weapon is aimed straight at him, no one can save him,
His father will not stand by him at court,
His own brothers will not vouchsafe for him at the word of the judge,
He is caught, unwittingly, in a bronze trap.
95 You blunt the horns of the man who commits sacrilege,
He who covets doing injustice, his firm ground *is shifted*.
You make the crooked judge taste of prison himself,
You make the one who accepts presents and yet denies justice suffer punishment.

The first line of Part II contains a finite verb in the second person, "You shepherd all those who are endowed with breath" (25); Part II continues up to its end, clearly delimited by the last occurrence of second-person forms addressing the sun in lines 97 and 98, with the same construction, for instance, "You keep crossing the sky faithfully" (27), "You pass over the wide earth every day" (28), and so on, up to "You make the one who accepts presents and yet denies justice suffer punishment" (98). As we have seen, the last four lines of Part I contain, beside nominal constructions, some second-person forms—"you oversee the earth" (line 21) and "You care for all peoples . . ." (line 23); lines 21-24 thus form the transition between the static first part and the second part which addresses the sun as a god who acts in the affairs of the world.

In this part of 78 lines, constituted by lines 21 through 98, there are altogether 36 second-person forms; in Akkadian, they are marked by the verb prefixes *ta-* or *tu-*, since the pronoun corresponding to English "you" ("thou") is implicit in the verb form. If we add to the verb forms formally marked by the prefix *t-* those two whose subject is the blaze or the face of the sun—"O Sun, your blaze descends even to the underground waters (line 37), and "You toil every day, your face never darkens" (line 41)—which are marked as referring to the sun addressed not on the verbs but on the grammatical subjects "blaze" and "face" by the suffix *-ka* "your," then the number of verb forms with second person referent rises to 38.

This part, then, is delimited from the preceding and, as we shall see, from the following parts by the predominance of one set of forms, namely second-person forms. Yet such a stretch of 78 lines seems too long for a single structural unit of the poem. Upon closer inspection, we find that, without relinquishing its emphasis on the sun as the actor, Part II is indeed broken up by the occurrence of two shorter units, one of eighteen lines (39-56) and another of fifteen lines (82-96) which are characterized by nominal predicates of the kind that were predominant in Part I. These shorter units articulate the 78 lines into four more easily apprehensible sections. The formal mark of these stative predicates is the ending *-ta,* the suffixal counterpart to the *t-* prefix of the second-person finite verbal forms.

In the first unit, lines 39-56, the forms *kasâta* "you tie" and *katmāta* "you cover" in line 39, *dalpāta* "you labor sleeplessly" (44), *naṭlāta* "you observe" (50) are such second-person statives; as the translations indicate, they cannot be rendered by a comparable construction in English. Of the two other statives—not marked with the second-person *-ta* ending because they are marked on their subject with the ending *-ka* "your"—namely "your fearsome sheen covers the land" (48) and "your broad protection is spread over all lands" (40), the latter alone could be rendered by the continuous form "is spread" as were the similar forms of Part I.

In the second unit, lines 82-96—much of it fragmentary—the phrases *sirāta* "you are majestic" (82), and *tarsat šetka* "your net is stretched" (87) lend themselves to this more literal translation with "are . . ." or "is . . ." These two nominal predicates alone refer to the sun in this second unit. The remaining statives, in "A twisted snare *is readied* for him" (90), "He *is caught,* unwittingly, in a bronze trap" (94), and "He who covets doing injustice, his firm ground *is shifted*" (96)—a line difficult to interpret—refer to some person who is identified only by some action characterizing him, a person "out there," a person in the world over which the sun has now risen.

The world that the sun is slowly illuminating as it climbs higher and higher has just intruded into the poet's consciousness, which has thus far been directed toward the contemplation and adoration of the sun itself; now we are ready to look at the world beneath the sun.

Thus Part II too has a transitional section toward its end, a transition from second-person to third-person forms. In fact, not only the three statives of lines 90-96, but already the verb forms "he will [. . .]" (89), "will not stand by him" (92), and "will not vouchsafe for him" (93), that is, six forms altogether, refer to the action of the people whom the sun—and with him the poet—sees from on high. The transitional section may have begun even before line 89, the line with the partly broken third-person predicate "he will [. . .]"; the fragmentary state of lines 75-90 prevents a more precise determination of the place where third-person forms set in. The fragmentary lines' reference to persons populating the world are phrased as participles (translated here by relative clauses) or as relative clauses without antecedent; the subjects thus remain unspecified. Nor do these unspecified people as yet engage in a particular activity; for lack of finite verb forms that would describe their actions only their general character emerges: "He who [. . .] to the oath" (line 85), "who does not fear [. . .]" (line 86), "he who coveted the wife of his partner" (line 88), and so on. Only in Part III, with the introduction of verbs to describe the activities carried out in society, does the world come into view as acting and interacting with the sun.

Part III comprises lines 99 through 125.

Part III

99 He who accepts no present and still intercedes for the weak
100   Is pleasing to the Sun, he will prolong his life.
    The conscientious judge who hands down a just verdict
        Has authority in the palace, his abode is that of princes.
    The moneylender who duns (the debtor)—what profit has he?
        As much as he counts on gain, he loses his capital.
105 The moneylender who lends on long term and takes no more than
        two shekels for one
    Is pleasing to the Sun, he will prolong his life.
    He who holding the scales weighs dishonestly,
        Substitutes weights, raises and lowers (the scales),
        As much as he counts on gain, he loses [his capital].
110 The honest man who holds the scales has many [. . .],
        All sorts of benefits are bestowed on him, [. . .].
    He who holds the bushel and measures dishonestly,
        Lends in the medium measure but collects in the large one,
    Will suffer men's curse before his time is up,
115   Will be called to reckoning before it is due, and suffer *punishment*.
    His heir will not succeed to his property,
        His brothers will not enter his household.
    The just creditor who gives barley by the large bushel increases his
        good fortune,
    Is pleasing to the Sun, he will prolong his life,

120 Will enlarge his family, acquire riches,
    Like water from a perennial spring, his descendants will be perennial.
    To one who is benevolent and innocent of guile
    ⟨line omitted?⟩
    Who constantly disguises his intentions—his case is before you.
    Those who do evil, their descendants will not [be perennial].
125 Those whose word is no—his case is before you.

I have said that I considered line 98 as the last line of Part II because the distich consisting of lines 97 and 98 contains the last pair of second-person forms until line 126. In Part III there is not a single second-person form. All finite verbs are in the third person: "The conscientious judge who hands down a just verdict" (101); "As much as he counts on gain, he loses his capital" (104); and so on; there is a total of eighteen third-person finite verbs in the twenty-seven lines of this part. The sun is mentioned only obliquely: in the idiomatic phrase "is pleasing to the sun" which recurs three times (lines 100, 106, and 119) and in the twice-occurring hemistich "his case is before you" (lines 123 and 125) where the suffix -*ka* denotes a second-person referent.

The last two distichs (122-123 and 124-125), both ending with the "his case is before you" hemistich, occur just before the reintroduction of second-person verb forms in Part IV and thus again form a transition to the next part.

This third part, only slightly longer than the first, is centrally placed in the poem, and is of central importance to its message. It is also the section that has received most attention from scholars of ancient Mesopotamia, because it can be construed as a code of ethics. This is the part which opposes the honest practitioners of several professions to their dishonest counterparts. The dishonest suffer the sun's punishment; the honest, just, and merciful are pleasing to the sun and obtain long life. The professions or estates singled out are few, but they all carry out a social function that gives them power over the poor and oppressed, that is, those members of society whose welfare, along with that of the widow and the orphan, have been the concern of legislators from the Sumerian king Urukagina (ca. 2350 B.C.) and the Babylonian king Hammurapi to Darius and to the precepts and parables of the Old and New Testaments. They are: the judge, the moneylender, the merchant, and the lender of that basic source of subsistence, barley; there is also another, unspecified category of persons, of whom it is only said that one is a benefactor and sincere, and the other, opposed to him, an evildoer and hypocrite. As just mentioned, concern for the poor and for those who have no powerful protector is a recurring topos in ancient texts, but we are concerned here with the exploitation of this topos in this particular poem. We may compare the lines that pit the person who weighs dishonestly against the one who does not (107-111), which must refer to the merchant, though he is not so named ("He who holding the scales weighs dishonestly, substitutes weights, raises and lowers (the scales)," etc.), to a passage from a Hittite hymn to the sun, in which the Hittite king complains:

> The merchant is a man who holds the scales under the sun and falsifies the scales—
> But I, what have I done to displease my god?[5]

In the Babylonian hymn to the sun, the distichs describing the dishonest practitioner are immediately followed by antithetic distichs describing the honest practitioner. The parallelism of the antithetical strophes is not uniform; the crooked judge has one distich for himself (lines 97-98), while two distichs are devoted to the rewards of the honest judge (lines 99-102). The harsh and the lenient moneylender each receive one distich; of the two merchants, the dishonest one is described in a three-line strophe, while the honest one again has one distich. As for the lender of barley, the dishonest creditor's fate is dwelt on in three distichs, and the fair creditor's in two. The parallelism, strict in its ordering of the dishonest first and the honest second, is thus tempered by variety in length and distribution. The varying lengths of these strophes not only introduce a variety in the parallelism, but also, in their diversity, create vignettes about the walks of life enumerated. Yet the lesson drawn from all these practices is underscored by the refrain-like repetition of the moral: "He is pleasing to the sun, he will prolong his life" which recurs in three of the four antithetic strophes (lines 100, 106, and 119); it is omitted only in the section concerning the merchant. Nor was the Old Testament mentioned casually in this connection: not only do these vignettes recall, with their epigrammatic sayings about man's estate, the Books of Wisdom, we actually find there a literal echo of the Šamaš hymn's phrase "what profit has he?" (line 103) in "What profit hath a man of all his labor which he taketh under the sun?" (Eccl. 1, 3) and "What profit hath he" (Eccl. 3, 9, 5, 16, and similar 2, 22); what was applied to the moneylender alone in the Hymn to the Sun is used as a refrain in Ecclesiastes.

The last two distichs of Part III have reference to some vague benefactor and evildoer, and thus, while still maintaining the structure of antithetical distichs, depart from the concrete descriptions of the preceding twenty-five lines, as if to give a more abstract summary of them. They are also the ones which reintroduce the sun as addressee with "his case is before you" in lines 123 and 125. The sun, depicted as the observer and dispenser of justice in Part III, here again becomes the divinity to whom the hymn is addressed, through the reintroduction of the suffix -*ka* heralding the return to second-person forms. The second-person forms, which were entirely absent from Part III, return in lines 126 and following, thus clearly demarcating the beginning of Part IV. Not only do second person verb forms return in these lines, they return with a vengeance: two in line 126 and three in line 127, five altogether in the two lines that both close a three-line strophe and open the next, fourth part:

Part IV

126   You press them to speak, you *clarify* it,
        You listen to men, discern them, you discern (the merit of) the case of the *wronged*.
    Each and every person is entrusted to your hands,
        You make the liver omens concerning them come out right, you undo what is tied fast.
130   You hear, O Sun, prayer, supplication, and homage,
        Prostration, kneeling, whispered prayer, and adoration.
    With constricted throat the feeble calls to you,
        The simple-minded, the weak, the wronged, the poor,
    Daily, regularly, constantly prays to you.
135   Whosoever's family is far away, whosoever's city is distant,
        The shepherd amidst the *terror* of the steppe prays to you.
    The shepherd boy in distress, the herder among the enemy,
        The caravan passing through a terrifying terrain prays to you, O Sun.
    The itinerant merchant, the apprentice who carries the weight pouch
140   The net-casting fisherman prays to you, O Sun.
    The hunter, the beater who rounds up the game,
        Behind the screen the fowler prays to you.
    He who slinks stealthily is also a petitioner of the Sun,
        On the tracks of the steppe the vagabond turns to you.
145   The roving dead, the lost soul
        Have prayed to you, Sun, you heard all.
    You have not *disdained* those who prayed to you, you were concerned about them;
        For my sake, O Sun, do not reject them!
    You grant knowledge, O Sun, to all humans,
150   You give them your fierce . . . , violent . . .
        You make their divination come out right, you are present in the sacrifice,
    You reveal their future as far as the four winds.
    You grant knowledge to the entire extent of the inhabited world.
    The heavens do not measure up to the *bowl* into which you look,
155   All the lands do not measure up to the oil-bowl of the diviner.
    On the Twentieth Day you rejoice, exult, and make merry,

You eat, you drink their pure drink-offering, beer bought from
the tavern-keeper,
You accept the tavern-keeper's beer when they libate it to you.
Those whom dangerous floodwater surrounds you save indeed,
160   You always receive from them their pure and sacred scattered
offerings.
You drink their mixed beer,
You let them attain the wish they have desired.
Those who . . . you release their . . . .
Those who have regularly said blessings to you, you have regularly
received their prayers.
165 As for them, they revere you, they praise your name constantly,
They proclaim your greatness forever.
Scoundrels and informers, who speak treachery,
Who, like the clouds, are beyond recording,
Those who pass along on the broad earth,
170   Those who tread the high mountains,
The monsters of the sea which are full of fearsomeness,
The yield of the sea which passes along the *apsû*,
The produce of the sea which passes *in review* before you, O Sun.
What mountains are not clad in your rays?
175 What regions do not bask in your bright light?

    In this fourth part, of 50 lines, there is an alternation of second-person forms, whose subject is the sun, and third-person forms, which refer to various people living under the sun who turn to him. The alternation of these forms brings the sun described in Part II, and the people living under the sun, enumerated in Part III, together into a dialectic of interaction of the world with the sun. Now the sun reaches into the world actively: "You press them to speak, you clarify it" (126); "You listen to men, discern them, you discern (the merit of) the case of the wronged" (127); "You make the liver omens concerning them come out right, you undo what is tied fast" (129); "You hear, O Sun, prayer, supplication, and homage" (130); "you heard all" (146); "You have not disdained those who prayed to you, you were concerned about them" (147); "You grant knowledge, O Sun, to all humans" (149); "you give them your fierce . . . , violent . . ." (150); and so on, throughout lines 151-153, 157-164; in addition, line 156, while it contains no finite second-person verb, has three statives in the second person (all marked by the suffix -*(ā)ta: rešāta illāta u hidāti* "You rejoice, exult, and make merry."
    These addresses to the sun cluster, as shown above, at the beginning of this part, in lines 126-130, which contain eight second-person forms, and again in lines 146-164, which contain eighteen. Between these two

groups and at the very end of Part IV two clusters of third-person forms describe, as mentioned, the world. The first of these clusters, lines 132-146, contains eight such third-person forms, and the second, lines 165-175, seven third-person forms and, in addition, four statives and one participle, all referring to the world, its people, and even its monsters.

These antiphonic groups, of respectively six, fifteen, nineteen, and eleven lines, in that order (those lines in which both second- and third-person forms occur are counted twice), also serve to articulate this part of the poem which, although shorter than the seventy-eight-line Part II, with its fifty lines is still longer than Parts I, III, V, or VI. These four groups form four sections within Part IV comparable to the four sections of Part II.

The third part of the poem described the just and the unjust with reference to their actions toward their fellow men. In the fourth part, all the mentioned people, coming from various walks of life, are viewed solely in relation to the sun; the verbs that refer to them all have the suffix *-ka* 'you' attached: these men address the sun, whom the poet also addresses thereby. More precisely, apart from the verb *išassika* 'calls to you' in line 132, all the verbs in lines 132-146 (the second section) are various forms of the verb *mahāru*—six in the present tense singular, translated as 'prays to you,' and one in the past tense plural, 'have prayed to you' (line 146). This repetition of the same lexical item is further reinforced by both the symmetry and the asymmetry of its placement: symmetry if we consider the first two and the last two distichs, where it is placed at the end of the line, and the middle two distichs, where it is placed at the beginning of the line, immediately after the vocative 'O Sun'; asymmetry if we contrast the two external pairs of distichs with the two middle ones. An inversion of word order, such as that which occurs in the middle distichs but which the constraints of English syntax make impossible to render in the translation, always highlights the line where it is placed; it is a marked feature of Akkadian syntax.

The second cluster of the verbs referring to people, the fourth and last section of Part IV (lines 165-175), contains a greater diversity both in grammatical form and in choice of lexical items. Apart from third-person finite verbs, we find statives: *palhaka* 'they revere you' (165), *la išā pana u bāba* 'are beyond recording (168), 'are full of fearsomeness' (171), 'are not clad in your rays' (174), and one participle: *dābibu ṣalipti* 'speaking treachery' (167). The seven finite verbs (e.g., 'they praise your name constantly' (165), 'they proclaim your greatness' (166)) all differ; only one, *ibâ'u* 'pass along,' is repeated in lines 169 and 172. There is also greater diversity in the way these predicates refer to the sun. Instead of adding the simple suffix *-ka* 'to you' to each, as in 'calls to you' and in the repeated 'prays to you' in lines 132-146, only one adds this suffix: 'they revere you' (165); four, although formally expressing the relation to the sun with the same suffix -*ka*, add it to the noun which is the verb's object: 'your name' (165), 'your greatness' (166), 'your rays' (174), 'your bright light' (175); and seven verbs have no reference to the sun at all ("those who pass along the broad earth, those who tread the high mountains," etc.). Yet another construction uses the adverbial phrase 'before you' (173), the same phrase that signaled the transition from Part III to Part IV, as pointed out above. In this position, toward the end of Part IV, it again serves the transitional function of leading away from the teeming multitudes into the next part, where the sun is again pictured as distant and no longer intervening in the affairs of the world, and wherein, as we shall see, the more contemplative mood of the beginning of the poem returns.

Indeed, with line 176, we find again the participial construction that characterized Part I. Lines 174-175 introduce this Part V both by their syntax and by their choice of words: "What mountains are not clad in your rays? What regions do not bask in their bright light?"; two lines— the only ones of the poem—which are couched in the form of questions. These lines also revert to the words 'rays, light' that studded the first part; they signal the focusing of attention on the light- and heat-bestowing aspect of the sun, and not any longer on his role as omniscient god. The light and heat attributes are again described in this fifth and next-to-last part by atemporal participles, ten in the first six lines.

Part V

176 Lightener of darkness, illuminator of obscurity,
Dispeller of shadows, illuminator of the broad earth,
Brightener of the day, who makes noonday heat descend upon the earth at midday,
Who scorches the broad earth like a flame,
180 Shortener of the days, lengthener of the nights,
Bringer of cold, frost, ice, and snow,
[   ] of the lock of heaven, who opens wide the doors of the habitations,
[   ] of lock, peg, key, latch,
[   ] does not forgive, granter of life,
185 [   ] the deported in the confusion, in the midst of death,
Deliberation, discussion, counsel,
[   ] . . . mornings to the far-flung peoples,
[   ] throne and reign [   ]
(189-192 broken)

Thus, while the structural scheme of Parts I and V is alike, and even some of the same participles occur in both, such as Illuminator (1, 3, 17, and 176, 177) and Brightener (4 and 178), the thematic content of the two differs. This is already indicated by the objects of the participles, which in Part V are not the same as those in Part I. In Part I it is the rising sun that illuminates the entire heavens; in Part V, it is the sun at its summer zenith that illuminates the wide earth and in addition brings the noonday heat, burning the wide earth as with fire. The sun is here followed not on its daily course but on its yearly cycle as it goes through the seasons from summer to winter:

> "Shortener of the days, lengthener of the nights,
> Bringer of cold, frost, ice, and snow." [6]

Since the last lines of the poem are fragmentary, it is not certain where Part V ends and where Part VI, the final doxology to the sun, begins. This last part has its predicates in the optative; the first certain one occurs in line 196.

Part VI

```
193   The bright [           ] is the dwelling of your rejoicing,
          [          ] banquet for all regions.
195   [Let ... ] governor, ruler, and prince
          [          ] bring you their tribute.
      [          ] in the sacrifice, the produce of all lands
      [          ] let your sanctuary be endlessly renewed,
      [          ] whose pronouncement cannot be changed
200   May [your] spouse [Aja . . .] say to you in the bedchamber: ["Be
              appeased."]
```

The wishes are addressed to the sun, exhorting the world to worship the sun and to bring him offerings, and the gods themselves to speak a blessing for him.[7]

Just as the sun was viewed under its double aspect, that of illuminator of the world and regulator of the seasons in the two outer parts and that of all-seeing dispenser of justice to the world in the three central parts, the world too is seen first as individuals or classes of people (in Parts II and III) and then as mankind as a whole, in Part IV. At the beginning of Part IV we still distinguish the wronged and the feeble, the shepherd, the merchant, the fisherman, the hunter; in the second half, from line 146 on, the sun's power and influence affects men in general or the inhabited world as a whole: "those who prayed to you"; "all humans"; "the inhabited world." This ecumenic aspect is underscored by the repeated occurrence of the word "all"; *kalama* (146), *kal* (153). The most common verb in this part is the verb *maharu*, which is used in two meanings: seven times in the first half in the meaning "pray to you," and three times (158, 160, 164) in the second half with the sun addressed as its subject in the meaning "you receive." In the first half, it was the people who turned to the sun; in the second half, the sun receives for himself prayers (158, 164) as well as offerings (160). Indeed, the sun eats and drinks (157, 161) the offerings presented to him and is described, with four second-person stative forms—one in line 151, and three in a row in line 156—as enjoying these offerings.

The end of Part IV thus leads away from the particular scenes depicted earlier, from the individual distresses or dishonesties which called forth the sun's response, and prepares us for the more cosmic view sketched in Part V. The sun's power and influence manifesting itself over the seasons cannot be apprehended at any single moment, and can be envisioned only when we distance ourselves from the individual and the ephemeral, from the immediate burden of the day.

We have seen how the repetitions of certain words achieve their particular effects in their similarity and in their difference, as those of the verb *maharu*. Yet, this verb occurs only three times with the sun as subject. Of all the verbs which have the sun as subject the one which occurs with the greatest frequency, even greater than the verb *maharu*, is, perhaps not surprisingly, the verb *tukallam* 'you show,' 'you bring to light.' It occurs four times, in lines 71, 72, 73, 97, that is, at the very center of the poem and indeed expresses the very nature of the sun, the same attribute the German ballad expresses as "Die Sonne bringt es an den Tag."[8]

In our presentation we have given special weight to the different verb forms—participles, statives, second- and third-person forms. Conspicuously absent among these is the first person, the voice of the poet. This person intrudes in the poem only once, in line 148, which begins with "For my sake." This unique occurrence is moreover given special emphasis by its line-initial position, immediately before the invocation "O Šamaš." Who the speaker is must remain unknown since Babylonian poets remain, with rare exceptions, anonymous.

NOTES

1. Translated by J. A. Wilson, ANET, pp. 369-71.

2. See in general F. J. Dölger, *Sol salutis* (Münster, 1925^2).

3. Charles Witke, *Numen Litterarum* (Brill: Leiden and Köln 1971), p. 129.

4. A similarly poetic description of the sun's course is found in the Book of Enoch, chapter 72, especially verse 37: ". . . it does not diminish (in brightness) and

it does not rest, but travels day and night," in O. Neugebauer, *The 'Astronomical' Chapters of the Ethiopic Book of Enoch (72 to 82)* (Kong. Danske Videnskabernes Selskab, Matematisk-fysiske Meddelelser 40:10), Copenhagen: Munksgaard 1981, p. 9.

     5. Hans G. Güterbock, "The Composition of Hittite Prayers to the Sun," JAOS 78 (1958) 237-245; idem, in *Altorientalische Literaturen*, ed. W. Röllig, (= *Neues Handbuch der Literaturwissenschaft*, Vol. 1) Wiesbaden: Akademische Verlagsgesellschaft Athenaion (1978), p. 229.

     6. Compare the Book of Enoch (see note 4) chapter 72, verse 15: "Then the sun sets out to shorten the day and to lengthen the night," Neugebauer, op. cit. p. 7.

     7. G. R. Castellino, in "The Šamaš Hymn: A Note on Its Structure," AOAT 25 (1976) 71-74, has noted the parallelism of the poem's beginning and end, though for him "the daily course of the Sun in his ascent into the skies" described in the first part corresponds to the sun's "return journey through the regions of the Netherworld" of the poem's end. It is interesting to note that his division of the hymn, on thematic grounds, into seven sections more or less coincides with my division based on linguistic as well as thematic criteria. To my Part III (lines 99-125) corresponds his pivotal Section IV (95-129), "Šamaš at his zenith"; he divides the sun's ascent into Section I "Šamaš at rise" (5-34), Section II "Šamaš starts on his onward march" (35-64), and Section III "Šamaš as Traveller through the skies" (65-94), sections which correspond to the here proposed Parts I (1-24) and II (25-96). He divides "Part II," the "return journey," into Sections V (130-155), VI (151-181), and VII (182-200), divisions roughly corresponding, with some overlap, to the here proposed Parts IV (126-175), V (176-192(?)), VI (193(?)-200).

     8. Adalbert von Chamisso, "Die Sonne bringt es an den Tag," Lieder und lyrisch-epische Gedichte (itself quoting "Die klare Sonne bringt's an den Tag" from Grimm's Märchen vol. II no. 29.

Chapter V

LYRIC POETRY

1. AN ASSYRIAN ELEGY

Little known, and the object of less attention, secular or folk poetry is hidden away in odd places within cuneiform literature. Unlike religious or learned poetry, it was not copied and recopied by the ancient scribes for study or cultic use. Yet some of the folk poetry can be recaptured, embedded as it is in magical texts as charms to be recited in the elaborate procedure uniting magic and medicine carried out by the practitioner of these arts for the healing of a patient. These charms, as can be expected, have affinities in content and form with the folk poetry of many cultures. They are our only evidence for positing for Babylonia too an oral poetry of an inspiration and *facture* quite distinct from the religious poetry to which the ancients as well as modern scholars have given the greater attention.

The two examples of secular poetry I have chosen reflect two different moods and two different traditions. The poem about the "heart grass," my second example, is one of a small number of short poems that can be assumed to preserve a folkloristic flavor. Different, and even unique, is the Assyrian Elegy, in that it belongs neither to the category of religious poetry nor to that of folk poetry. The title I have given it is descriptive only of its language—Assyrian—and its tone. Otherwise, its place in Mesopotamian literature is not known, because it is written by itself on a clay tablet without any title, rubric, or reference to liturgical or other performance, such as often help to situate other poems. Its unique character may be due solely to the chance of discovery; still, as it is written in the Assyrian dialect, we may assume that it represents a specifically Assyrian sensitivity and poetic inspiration that was not favored in the poetic circles of Babylonia and thus not preserved in our predominantly Babylonian literary corpus. Of the single copy we possess,[1] a small portion is broken away, depriving us of the beginnings of seven lines. Contrary to most instances where such partially broken lines can be restored with reasonable confidence since there exist many texts of similar diction, this poem cannot be restored completely. The general tenor and structure are nevertheless clear.

1 ana mīni kî eleppê ina qabal nārê nadâki
   a-na me-i-ni ki-i GIŠ.MÁ-e ina MURUB₄ ÍD-e na-da-ki

2 šabburu hūqikî battuqu ašliki
   šab-bu-ru hu-qi-ki-i ba-tu-qu áš-li-ki

3 kallulu panikî nār Libbi āli tebbiri?
   ka-lu-lu pa-ni-ki-i ÍD URU.ŠÀ.URU te-bi-ri

4 akê la nadākû la battuqu ašliya?
   a-ke-e la na-da-ku-ú la ba-tu-qu áš-li-iá

5 ina ūme inbu aššûni akê hadāka anāku
   ina u₄-me in-bu áš-šu-u-ni a-ke-e ha-da-ka a-na-ku

6 hadāk anākû hadi hābirî
   ha-da-ak a-na-ku-ú ha-di ha-bi-ri-i

7 ina ūme hilūyâ ētarpû paniya
   ina u₄-me hi-lu-ia-a e-tar-pu-u pa-ni-ia

8 ina ūme ulādiya ittakrima ēnāya
   ina u₄-me ú-la-di-ia it-ta-ak-ri-ma IGI^II.MEŠ-ia

9 patâni upnāyâ ana Bēlet-ilî uṣalla
   pa-ta-ni up-na-ia-a a-na ᵈBe-let-DINGIR ú-ṣal-la

10 'ummu ālidāte attî eṭirî napultî!'
   um-mu a-li-da-te at-ti-i e-ṭi-ri-i na-pu-ul-ti

11 Bēlet-ilî kî tašmūni tuktallila paniša
   ᵈBe-let-DINGIR.MEŠ ki-i ta-áš-mu-ni tuk-tal-li-la pa-ni-šá

12 '[   ] attî ana mēni tuṣṣanallini?'
   [a]t-ti-i a-na me-ni tu-ṣa-na-li-ni

1 "Why are you adrift, like a boat, in the midst of the river,

2 your thwarts in pieces, your mooring rope cut?

3 Your face covered, you cross the river of the Inner City."

4 "How could I not be adrift, how could my mooring rope not be cut?

5 The day I bore the fruit, how happy I was,

6 happy was I, happy my husband.

7 The day of my going into labor, my face became darkened,

8 the day of my giving birth, my eyes became clouded.

9 With open hands I prayed to Bēlet-ilī:

10 'You too have borne a child, save my life!'

11 Hearing this, Bēlet-ilī veiled her face.

12 'You [...], why do you keep praying to me?'

13 [-m]ūni ittidî riganšu
   [-m]u?-u-ni it-ti-di-i ri-ga-an-šú

14 '[   ]ni aššat laliyâ'
   [   ]-ni áš-šat la-li-ia-a

15 [   ] ša dūr šanātê
   [   ] ša du-ur MU.AN.NA.MEŠ-e

16 [   ] ša qaqqar hibilāte
   [   ] ša-a qaq-qar hi-bi-la-te

17 [   ] Libbi-āli . . . tassisî nubû
   [URU].ŠÀ.URU RI ŠID ta-si-si-i nu-bu-u

18 [   ] ūmē annûte issi hābiriya anāku
   [   ] UD.MEŠ an-nu-te TA ha-bi-ri-ia a-na-ku

19 issišu ašbākû ša rāimāniya
   is-si-šu áš-ba-ku-ú ša ra-i-ma-ni-ia

20 mūtu ina bīt mayāliya ihlulâ hillutu
   mu-u-tú ina É.KI.NÁ-ia ih-lu-la-a hi-il-lu-tú

21 issu bītiyâ ussēṣanni yāši
   TA É-ti-ia-a us-se-ṣa-an-ni a-a-ši

22 issu pan hābiriya iptarsanni yāši
   TA pa-an ha-bi-ri-ia ip-tar-sa-an-ni a-a-ši

23 šēpēya issakana ina qaqqar la . . . tiya
   GÌR^{II}.MEŠ-ia is-sa-ka-na ina qaq-qar la x-x-ti-iá

13   [My husband, who loved me], uttered a cry,

14   ['Why do you take from me] the wife in whom I rejoice?'

15   [   ] years on end,

16   [   ] ......

17   [   ] Inner City , ... you sounded a wail.

18   [All] those [many] days I was with my husband,

19   I lived with him who was my lover.

20   Death came creeping into my bedroom:

21   it drove me from my house,

22   it tore me from my husband,

23   it set my feet into a land of ....

This elegy is a brief poem compared to the 200-line Hymn to the Sun or even to considerably shorter religious poems. It has but 23 lines, and there are no rulings to divide them into stanzas or distichs. Its structure emerges only as we read the alternating parts of the dialogue. For the inner structure of the elegy is that of a dialogue, or better, a sequence of dialogues within a dialogue. No formal features set off the alternating parts, as happens in other poems written in dialogue form—the Babylonian Theodicy, the disputations, and others—in which two interlocutors take turns and in which the speeches of one are set off from the other's by rulings on the tablet. The outer dialogue consists of a question and an answer; the question takes up the first three lines and the answer the rest of the poem, twenty lines. This structure, not unlike the rhetorical device of the speaker answering his own question, brings to mind such famous examples as "Shall I compare thee to a summer's day?" and "Kennst du das Land, wo die Zitronen blüh'n?," lyric poems, like ours; real dialogues usually appear in narrative poems such as ballads and, of course, epics.

Within this outer frame of question-and-answer at least one further dialogue is embedded in the answer part of the poem, and possibly two. How many there are must emerge from the content alone since none of the interlocutors is introduced by the standard formula "so-and-so started to speak and addressed so-and-so" that articulates speeches in narrative poetry and that we encountered in the Descent of Ištar. Failing an introductory formula naming the speaker, we discover only gradually, as the poem unfolds, who it is that gives the long answer to the initial question; nor do we ever learn who it was that asked the question.

The changes of speakers are indicated in the embedded dialogue or dialogues only by such introductory phrases as "I prayed to" and "he uttered a cry" (and possibly one or two others, now broken); otherwise, only the alternations of first- and second-person verb forms, first- and second-person pronouns, and masculine and feminine forms clue us to the changes. There is, in addition, a formal characteristic that may have provided further clues to the ancient reader. The poem exhibits a spelling peculiarity in that some words contain an extra vowel sign that is motivated neither by the cuneiform writing conventions nor by grammatical reasons. This device can be seen in lines 2, 3, 4, etc., of the transliteration (however, the ki-i in line 1, the extra -u in line 5, and others, are required by spelling conventions). This spelling pattern is certain to have a function, even if we do not know what it is. It has been suggested that such extra-long vowels add to the elegiac tone;[2] other explanations are possible. The spelling perhaps endeavors to render a linguistic feature signalling, for example, that the speaker is a woman, as in the "women's dialect" of some languages, among them Sumerian.

If these spellings do not function as clues to the tenor, they may, on the phonetic level, indicate with the extra vowel syllables the rising intonation of the questions, as in hu-qi-ki-i (2), pa-ni-ki-i (3), na-da-ku-ú (4). Yet such syllables are added to personal suffixes in non-interrogative contexts too, as in hi-lu-la-ia-a (7), up-na-ia-a (9), la-li-ia-a (14), bīti-ia-a (21), ha-bi-ri-i (6); and to verb forms as well, forms not only of "weak" verbs where such a vowel may have some justification, as in it-ti-di-i (13) and ta-si-si-i (17), but of others, as in e-tar-pu-u (7), e-ṭi-ri-i (10), ih-lu-la-a (20).

Even if these syllables should contribute to the metrical scheme, their role is not immediately apparent, although metrical reasons for the presence of at least some of the extra vowel syllables can be adduced—but only if we consider syllable count relevant to metric structure, whereas Babylonian metrics is usually regarded as based on a fixed number of stresses. It is even possible that such a syllable count, where pertinent, was meant, like the rulings and caesuras in other poems, for the eye only. That there is a conscious patterning of sounds in the poem is apparent from such features as alliteration (*ha*dâk anākû *ha*di *hā*birí line 6), repetition of sounds (i*hlu*lâ *hillū*tu line 20, a*kê* la nadākû line 4, a*kê* hadāka line 5, ētar*pu pan*iya line 7, *pat*âni u*pnā*yâ line 9), and the numerous rhymes, not only at the ends of lines (in *-kī*, in *-ya*), but also internally (e.g., in lines 2, 7, 8, 10).

The feature of syntactic parallelism appears in the pairs of lines 7-8 and 21-22, as well as in the symmetrical two half-lines of line 6 and the three half-lines spread over line 2 and the first half of line 3. Since the beginnings of lines 12-18 are broken, in seven of the twenty-three lines we cannot ascertain the presence or absence of parallelism.

The translation can render the parallelism and other syntactic features, but not the linguistic or metric references of the spelling, and only rarely the sound patterns of the original (*c*ame *c*reeping, *h*ow *h*appy, *h*appy my *h*usband). It requires only a couple of explanatory glosses: the Inner City is the city of Assur; Bēlet-ilí, literally "Mistress of the gods," is a name for the mother goddess. Nor does the principal metaphor of the poem need special explanation: the metaphor of the boat adrift touches us too, conditioned as we are by Rimbaud's *"Bateau Ivre"* or Mallarmé's poem *"Brise Marine"* with *Perdus, sans mâts, sans mâts* in its final quatrain. It is indeed clear from the very first line that the image of the boat stands for the person addressed, even if this were not expressed by the wording of the simile *kī eleppe* 'like a boat'; one does not normally address questions to boats. But the simile turns immediately into metaphor: "Your thwarts," "your mooring rope"; and the metaphor of the boat, a word of feminine gender in Akkadian, identifies the person addressed as a woman.

The implications of the metaphor become even more apparent if we recall that in Mesopotamian literature the image of a boat seeking safe harbor is often associated with a child about to be born. An incantation for the safe delivery of a child refers to the unborn with the lines "The boat is held fast at the quay of death, the barge is held fast at the quay of suffering" and seeks to bring "The rope of the boat to the safe mooring place, the rope of the barge to the quay of life."[3] The reader of the elegy is thus prepared for the words "labor" and "giving birth" first introduced in lines 7 and 8. Before this explicit identification of the woman as a mother in childbed, there appears another, transitional metaphor: "the day I bore the fruit." The leap from boat to fruit, startling as it seems, is willingly accepted insofar as our expectations, aroused by the boat image, have included the association with childbirth; the fruit is, obviously, the newborn child, a metaphor often used as a personal name or part of one. Progressively, we identify the speaker first as a woman, and then as a woman who died in giving birth.

The lament of the woman includes a quote from a dialogue between herself, the dying mother, and the mother goddess. Her cry "You too have borne a child, save my life!" has been rendered somewhat freely; the first clause literally means "You are the mother of women who give birth"; yet a divine patron, mother, or father, is usually so identified because of the deity's own skill or experience. Bēlet-ilī is the "mother of women who give birth" because she herself has borne children, as she says in her complaint about the gods' plan to destroy mankind in the Flood, "It is I who give birth to these human beings of mine" (Gilgameš Tablet XI 122); also "I gave birth to all the Igigu gods" (JCS 31 103:47, Story of Anzû, Old Babylonian version, and ibid. 88 iv 4, Standard Babylonian version). The goddess is unable or unwilling to save her. "She has veiled her face," a gesture indicating that she does not receive the prayer. Her reasons, if they were expressed, are lost in the lacuna at the beginning of line 12.

In the next two lines the husband is introduced; even though the beginnings of the lines are missing, not only the preserved "the wife in whom I rejoice" of line 14, but already the masculine referent of "his cry" of line 13 indicate that another dialogue has begun; the addressee was most likely mentioned in line 14. (The restorations of the beginnings of the lines are free; the word-final syllables after the break indicate only that the first half of line 13 contains a relative clause, and the first half of line 14 probably ends with a verb form suffixed with "me" or "from me"). The husband's cry may have gone to the mother goddess, or even to Death personified, personified as he is in line 20.

The next two lines are too fragmentary to tell who is speaking; in line 17, the "you" again is feminine but it is not known what woman or goddess the dead woman addresses before she returns to bewailing her lost marital happiness. By the time the lament of the dead wife comes to an end, the initial image, that of the boat adrift, has receded, so that it is not incongruous that we find ourselves landlocked in the last line, with its words *šēpu* 'foot' and *qaqqaru* 'land'. The voice that spoke from beyond the tomb came, no doubt, from the Land of No Return.

NOTES

1. K.890, first published by S. A. Strong, in Beiträge zur Assyriologie 2 (1894) 634; new translation (in German) based on collation of the tablet, by E. Reiner in *Neues Handbuch der Literaturwissenschaft*, I. Altorientalische Literaturen, ed. W. Röllig (Wiesbaden: Athenaion, 1978), p. 186f. Another translation and photographs of the tablet are published by Rainer Albertz, *Persönliche Frömmigkeit und offizielle Religion* (Stuttgart: Calwar, 1978), p. 54 and following plate (Calwer Theologische Monographien 9).

2. See K. Deller, Orientalia NS 34 (1965) 464.

3. Cuneiform text in F. Köcher, Die babylonisch-assyrische Medizin, vol. III, No. 248 ii 51-52 and iii 58ff.

2. THE HEART GRASS

This poem never stood on its own, as did the Elegy. It was preserved in writing no doubt only because it was recited in connection with some magic manipulations and thus was included in the scholarly corpus of medical texts, in which it appears more than once. It illustrates not only the type of folk poetry that must have existed in oral tradition in Babylonia, but also the "almost universal forms of folk poetry" of which Edward Stankiewicz speaks: ". . . verse, the most pervasive and systematic of all formal devices, is not merely a structure of unfolding parallelisms of sound and meaning, but a system in which the parallelisms of form *serve to create* parallelisms of meaning. . . . [The] alternation of linguistic parallelism can be clearly observed in those almost universal forms of folk poetry which are built on 'syntactic parallelism' in which the syntactic resemblance of the lines is counterbalanced by lexical variation."[1]

The Heart Grass

1 šammu ša libbi ina šadî asīma assuhšuma issabat libbī
2 ana šamaš aqbīma issabat libbi šamaš
3 ana umāmi aqbīma issabat libbi umāmi
4 ana sēri u bamāti aqbīma issabat libbi sēri u bamāti
5 ana šadî u harrī aqbīma issabat libbi šadî u harrī
6 ana asalluhi bēlija bēl āšipūti aqbīma umma libbī lippašir
7 kīma libbī ippašir libbi šamaš lippašir
8 kīma libbi šamaš ippašir libbi umāmi lippašir
9 kīma libbi umāmi ippaširma libbi sēri u bamāti lippašir
10 kīma libbi sēri u bamāti ippaširma libbi šadî u harrī lippašir
11 šamaš šammu annû šammaka šātīšu liblut
12 šātīšu lišir šātīšu muršašu limtaššir šātīšu lišlim
13 šātīšu ēma usammaru likšud

The heart grass grows in the mountains; I pulled it up and it seized my heart.
I spoke to Šamaš—it seized the heart of Šamaš.
I spoke to the beasts—it seized the hearts of the beasts.
I spoke to the fields and plains—it seized the hearts of the fields and plains.
I spoke to the hills and vales—it seized the hearts of the hills and vales.

> I spoke to my lord Asalluhi, the lord of exorcism: Let my heart be soothed.
> As my heart is soothed, so may the heart of Šamaš be soothed.
> As the heart of Šamaš is soothed, so may the hearts of the beasts be soothed.
> As the hearts of the beasts are soothed, so may the hearts of the fields and plains be soothed.
> As the hearts of the fields and plains are soothed, so may the hearts of the hills and vales be soothed.
> O Šamaš, this grass is your grass: he who drinks it shall revive,
> He who drinks it shall recover, he who drinks it shall be rid of his illness, he who drinks it shall regain health,
> He who drinks it shall attain his desires.

The most complete exemplar occupies thirteen lines on a tablet with medical prescriptions.[2] The end of each line coincides with the end of a sentence, unlike the text on the remainder of the tablet. This feature alone shows that we have here no ordinary prose.

The beginnings of the lines are marked by sound repetition: the first line and the last three lines begin with *ša,* an alliterative sequence; the second through the sixth with *ana,* a preposition, and the seventh through the tenth with *kīma libbi,* a syntagm, and thus lines 7-10 constitute the figure called, in classical rhetoric, anaphora, that is, the figure where words are repeated at the beginnings of successive lines. Lines 6-10 are marked at the ends of the lines by the repetition of the same word *(lippašir),* a figure known as epiphora. Line 6, beginning with *ana* and ending with *lippašir,* forms the bridge between the sequences of anaphoric and epiphoric lines, and has the double function of closing the first sequence and opening the next.

The word repetitions in lines 2-10 are at the same time repeated occurrences of the same syntactic frames, one in lines 2-5 (*ana* X *aqbīma issabat libbi* X 'I spoke to X—it seized the heart of X') and the other in lines 7-10 (*kīma libbi* X *ippašir libbi* Y *lippašir* 'as the heart of X is soothed, so may the heart of Y be soothed'). Up to the middle of line 6 all lines are narrative; from the second half of line 6 on they contain a wish. Thus line 6 which contains the first half of the first syntactic frame and the second half of the second syntactic frame constitutes the midpoint of the poetic structure as it both divides and unites the two halves of the text on the sound level, the syntactic level, and the content level. It is also the only line in which the words "*Asalluhi,* the lord of exorcism," occur, and thus is thematically pivotal and reinforces the classification of the text as an incantation.

The first half of the text is narrated in the first person, with the exception of the first hemistich whose subject is the "heart grass." The second half similarly has a breaking point at line 11, which begins with a direct address to the god. Thus the first line, the introduction, and the last three lines, the coda—the same lines that, as we have seen, all begin with the alliterative sequence *ša*—form the frame of the poem, which goes from narration to prayer.

While the frame is asymmetrical, the two constituent sequences of the central section are completely symmetrical, divided as they are into two equal parts by the transitional line 6.

The poem's special feature is that it contains two compositional devices: syntactic parallelism in the first half and a concatenation in the second half. The parallelism may be represented by the frame

$$
\begin{array}{cccc}
a & x & b & x & c \\
a & y & b & y & c \\
a & z & b & z & c \\
a & w & b & w & c \\
\end{array}
$$

the variable items of which, x, y, z, w, are taken up in the concatenation so that instead of being repeated in each hemistich they are linked in the pattern xy, yz, zw as in a chain.

Such syntactic parallelisms, or chains without interrelation of members,[3] are otherwise unknown in Babylonian poetry, but examples of concatenations, or chains with interdependent members, as in the second half of our poem, do occur; it is especially noteworthy that this poem combines the two types of chains in such a way that the first chain introduces the elements of the second. The first frame: "I spoke to X, it seized the heart of X" is successively filled by the four nouns or phrases *Šamaš, umāmu, ṣēri u bamāti, šadî u harri*, in such a way that both slots of the lines are filled by the same noun or phrase. In a variant recension of this poem, only three items are substituted in the frame, indicating that the nature of such lists of items is that they can be expanded or reduced at will. In the second chain, the frame "As the heart of X is soothed, so may the heart of Y be soothed" is filled successively by the same list of items, but in such a way that the second item of the first line appears as the first element of the next line, and so forth, conforming with the rhetorical figure called anadiplosis. The closest comparable example to this second type of chain is the verse about the Horseshoe Nail:

> For want of a nail the shoe was lost,
> For want of a shoe the horse was lost,
> For want of a horse the man was lost,
> For want of a man the battle was lost.

Other incantations contain only the chain with interdependent members, and appear in a less elaborate form. The frame—the constant item—consists of a single word and even this single word may be omitted in the repetition so that only the variable items appear in the pattern xy, yz, zw, etc. Thus, of two variant versions of a little charm one contains the one-word frame "bore": "The earth bore the soil, the soil bore the stalk, the stalk bore the ear, the ear bore the ergot" and the other omits it once its function of connecting the successive items has been established both syntactically and semantically: "The plow bore the furrow, the furrow the germ, the germ the stalk, the stalk the ear, the ear the ergot."[4]

The end of the poem takes up three lines, which fall into one half-line and one two-and-a-half-line section. The half-line section contains an invocation to the god, an address typical of incantations and prayers. The second section contains five wishes for the speaker's welfare. This ending itself places the poem in the religious or magic genre; indeed, it was so classified by the ancients who gave it the title "incantation," and provided it with the standard incantation formula.

The final section's five wishes are connected by the identical word *šatīšu* repeated at the beginning of each, by their syntactic parallelism, and by their sound pattern. Their variable elements—the five verbs in the optative that conclude them—get longer, with one exception, from one phrase to the next, an expected feature of Akkadian syntax, since coordinate members of a sequence are typically so enumerated that the longest one stands in the last place. They go from (1) *libluṭ* to (2) *līšir*, (3) *murṣašu limtaššir*, (4) *lišlim* and finally (5) *ēma usammaru likšud*. The first is standard in prayers and is often paired with the one that here stands in the fourth place, such as *lubluṭ lušlim* (in first-person formulation) "may I get well, may I be safe." These two standard phrases are separated by a longer wish (3) which refers to physical well-being; the final and longest (5) is the most general and abstract.

The analysis of the formal properties of this poem was intended to lay the foundation for showing how this tightly knit structure is correlated with the manifestation of the main thrust of the poem at all linguistic levels.

To the two main themes, the attack of the disease and the deliverance from it, correspond the two main divisions of the poem. In the first part, the description of the attack is reinforced by the five-times repeated verb "seized"; in the second, the deliverance is underlined by the repetition, not once but twice in each line, nine times in all, of the key word "soothe." The poem begins with the key word *šammu*, reinforced by the alliteration *šammu ša libbi*. This key word does not recur again until the conclusion; instead, it is the word *libbu* "heart" which follows it that will be repeated throughout the central section, fourteen times in all. Where the litany-like repetition of *libbu* ceases, the word *šammu* is reintroduced, this time not with alliteration alone but with complete sound parallelism in *šamaš šamme annâ šammaka*.

The two main parts, with their sequences of four items depict, step by step, the continually expanding reach of the evil and likewise the deliverance expected, first through the parallelism of the syntactic frame of lines 2-5, and secondly in the chain of lines 7-10. This expansion begins at the speaker and progressively encompasses the world around him, from his god—close to him, as we see from the place accorded to the name Šamaš beside the pronoun referring to the speaker—to farther and farther ranges of the inhabited world around him: the animals of the pasture surrounding the city, the outlying fields and plains, and finally the mountains, wild mountains as their paired association with the word *harri* "mountain torrent" suggests. This pair, rendered in the translation by "hills and vales," a similar set pair in English, and thereby losing some of the connotations of the original, evoked for the Mesopotamian plain dweller remote and dangerous terrain, associated with foreign invasions or costly military and commercial ventures. As we reach this outer boundary of the speaker's world, we find ourselves back in the habitat of the grass, which was said, in the introduction, to grow in the mountains. The sequence has thus successfully presented the grass's habitat as the remote mountains, fraught with danger; to journey that far to pick the grass cannot but suggest that it must be endowed with special powers. Indeed, as we reach the conclusion of the poem, we learn that the grass is endowed with special powers by Šamaš, and that it will bring healing and success to him who drinks the potion.

The divisions of the poem are also apparent from its sound structure. The sounds *ša* that are repeated three times in the first line and mark one of the key words, *šammu,* suddenly are thrust upon us with an unparalleled frequency in the last three lines, beginning with line 11 which introduces the conclusion, in a half line which hardly contains any other sounds but those that make up the word *šammu: šamaš šamme annâ šammaka* (whether the incorrectness of the grammatical endings—the correct form would be *šammu annû šammaka*—has been occasioned by the desire to keep the sound parallelism more complete we cannot tell). The second key word, also introduced in the first line, *libbu* "heart," is not only repeated in the two main sections, once in each line of the first, and twice in each line of the second, but is also reinforced by the repetition of the syllable *lip* at the end of each line of the second section, to which the ending *libbī lippašir,* of the transitional line 6, forms the upbeat. The same syllable *lib* begins the second part of the conclusion, in the word *libluṭ.* Note that this word is the only one in the five cola that does not contain the most-insisted-upon sounds *š* and *m*. The remaining four cola again take up the sound parallelism not only with the repeated *šātišu* but also in the variable parts of the phrases. The colon that contains these sounds in the greatest profusion, *murṣašu limtaššir,* is thus marked, as it is on the semantic level also, as exceptional, not just as the only one of the five that is not otherwise known from similar formulas, but also as the one containing the word *murṣu* "sickness," obviously a key semantic notion of the poem but which appears here for the first and only time.

The perception of the linguistic structure is a necessary prerequisite for reading a poem on different levels. In a modern poem the reader is expected to perceive, moreover, the metaphorical dimensions and literary allusions, and to be able to shift from the literal to one or several possible metaphorical readings. The literary critic is often able to point out levels of understanding that are not always directly perceptible. For a poem in a dead language and echoing an alien thought, it devolves upon the philologist to suggest, on the basis of the knowledge available to him, some readings that go beneath the surface of the literal expression.

When the poem begins with *šammu ša libbi,* "the heart grass,"— words and sounds that, we have seen, echo throughout the poem—this expression denotes simply an herb, under a descriptive name the likes of which are common in technical texts such as plant lists compiled for pharmaceutical purposes. The compound term may be parsed in the Akkadian language either as "the herb *against* the heart," that is, affecting the heart, or as "the herb *for* the heart," that is, soothing the heart. As the first line of our poem ends, we have been directed to chose the first interpretation, "herb affecting the heart," because of the words *iṣṣabat libbi* "it seized my heart"; the first, *iṣṣabat,* often denotes the act of seizing as a malevolent act, something that diseases and demons do, and thus steers our imagination to the affliction, and the second, *libbī,* with the personal suffix "my" appended to "heart," points to a personal involvement. This reading is reinforced in the next four lines in which the words *iṣṣabat libbi* are repeated throughout. The interpretation that was equally possible, "herb *for* the heart," which we dismissed upon reaching the end of the first line, has, however, not yet had time to fade before it reemerges, prompted by the use of the verb *pašāru,* as the appropriate reading to be selected for line 6. I have translated this verb as "soothe"; it literally means "undo." Thus, the herb that gripped my heart will also undo the effects of the seizure; that which grieved my heart is also the plant that is to soothe my heart. By the time the chain ends and the address *Šamaš šammu annû šammaka,* "O Šamaš, this grass is your grass," is reached, there is no doubt left that the herb, the god's herb, is beneficial, and so the "heart grass," ambiguous at the beginning of the poem, has been indeed identified as the balm for the heart, bringing healing to body ("he who drinks it shall recover," etc.) and to mind and soul ("he who drinks it shall attain his desires").

At the moment there remain parts and allusions in the poem as yet without explanation. We do not know precisely to what experiences the beasts, hills and vales, fields and plains refer, and in lines 3 and 4 some emendations (based on the second occurrence of these items) were necessary to preserve the parallel structure—perhaps a line has dropped out from our version or two lines have been conflated. Our version may well be a truncated version of a longer poem, and the other recension, with the same structure but a shorter and somewhat different sequence: Šamaš, heaven and earth, beasts, may be another. Only acquaintance with the use of images throughout Babylonian poetry can help to elucidate not only the literal meaning but also the deeper levels of any one poem.

NOTES

1. Edward Stankiewicz, "Structural Poetics and Linguistics," in *Current Trends in Linguistics,* ed. T. A. Sebeok, vol. 12, *Linguistics and the Adjacent Arts and Sciences* (The Hague: Mouton, 1974), p. 649.

2. O. R. Gurney and P. Hulin, *The Sultantepe Tablets II* (London: The British Institute of Archaeology at Ankara, 1964), No. 252, lines 1-13; similar or somewhat shorter versions are preserved in F. Köcher, *Die babylonisch-assyrische Medizin,* vol. VI, No. 574 iii 34-39, and AO 7765 r. 8'-14', copied by Jean Nougayrol, "Tablettes diverses du Musée du Louvre," Revue d'Assyriologie 73 (1979) 69; an unpublished duplicate is K. 19455, transliterated by W. G. Lambert.

3. For the classifications "chain with interdependent members" and "chain without interrelation of members" see Stith Thompson, Motif-Index of Folk-Literature, vol. V (Indiana University Press, 1957), p. 543 Z30 and p. 546 Z40.

4. See Benno Landsberger and Thorkild Jacobsen, "An Old Babylonian Charm against *Merhu,"* JNES 14 (1955) 14-21, text on pp. 15-16, with corrections by Benno Landsberger, JNES 17 (1958) 56.

Chapter VI

"THIS YEAR AND INTO THE NEXT..."
THE SECOND TABLET OF *Ludlul bēl nēmeqi:*
INTRICATE TEXTURE OF A LEARNED POEM

The "Poem of the Righteous Sufferer," last edited, under this title, by W. G. Lambert in his *Babylonian Wisdom Literature* (Oxford: Clarendon Press 1960), is "an opus quite *sui generis* which was, at times, glibly misnomered the 'Babylonian Job' and is often ranged among the text category 'Wisdom Literature' but can perhaps be best characterized as an original creation of Mesopotamian religious lyrical poetry somehow akin in mood, scope, and setting to certain psalms. A princely sufferer describes first his afflictions which, caused by divine wrath and alienation, have broken him in body and spirit and brought him near death. At the very climax of his 'Passion' three successive dreams presage his impending return to grace and health. The balance of the poem then praises in hymnical style the saviour, Marduk, describing the gratefulness of the sufferer. The document offers a mine of information concerning religious concepts and practices in its elaborate descriptions of the physiological and psychological details of the symptoms of the sufferer. It furthermore sheds light upon the conflict between piety and the doubts of despair and reveals in this connection more about the intellectual and spiritual aspects of Mesopotamian religiosity than any other religious text with the exception of the so-called 'Theodicy.' "[1]

The "mine of information" concerning Mesopotamian religiosity intimated in this succinct characterization of the poem by A. L. Oppenheim has so far remained untapped.[2] Nor has its character as "religious lyrical poetry" been explored, possibly due to its length. It is, in fact, a long religious poem in praise of Marduk, as its incipit—which serves, as customary, as its title—states: *Ludlul bēl nēmeqi* 'Let me praise the Lord of Wisdom,' although some epic poems too begin with such hymnic introductions.[3] Like other prayers, it consists of a monologue describing the sufferings of the supplicant. It differs from prayers not only by its unusual length—it is inscribed on four tablets with 120 lines each, for a total of 480 lines—but mainly by the fact that it contains no petition—none is needed since for the narrator deliverance by Marduk, the Lord of Wisdom, has already taken place.

The first half of the poem—the first two tablets—describes the undeserved sufferings that beset the speaker. The third tablet recounts how a dream apparition, sent by Marduk, made him regain his health and his lost social position, and the fourth, only fragmentarily preserved, the pilgrimage of praise and thanksgiving undertaken by the man so saved.

That the moral problem of divine justice finds expression in this poem is only to be expected; I shall not dwell on it here since it has been the subject of numerous studies. The combination of this topic with a dream-figure savior is a feature unique to this poem, as was pointed out by Oppenheim. The triumphal entry into Babylon connects this poem with yet another genre: scholastic literature giving theological-philological interpretations of names of gods and temples; in this instance the names interpreted are those of the gates of Babylon's Marduk-temple, Esagil (see p. 112f.).

This ending in itself would betray that the poem is the work of a scholar, even if it were not the fact that it contains an unusual number of learned and rare words that the ancients found necessary to gloss and comment upon. Such commentaries are otherwise known only for scholarly texts, principally divinatory texts (from the realm of astrology, extispicy), medical texts and some rituals,[4] and lexical texts. Of literary works only one other text similar in subject matter and tenor, the so-called "Babylonian Theodicy," has been provided with a commentary, while the commentaries on the Poem of Creation *(Enūma eliš)* are mainly theological in nature.

The division of the poem into four tablets of equal length is artificial in terms of Babylonian conventions, though paralleled in European literature.[5] Babylonian texts are divided into "tablets"—for poetry we might call them "cantos"—according to the physical properties of the clay tablet which is the text's vehicle: its size, any divisions of its faces into two or more columns, and the size of the cuneiform signs used. A length of one hundred to two hundred lines is common; for example, the Poem of Creation has seven tablets of 162, 134+, 138, 146, 156, 166, and 162 lines respectively, and of the five tablets of the Epic of Irra the three fully preserved ones have 191 (Tablet I), 150 (Tablet IV), and 61 lines (Tablet V). The division of *Ludlul* into exactly 120-line tablets is obviously intentional and shows the same artifice as the choice of language; in this, *Ludlul* matches not the epic poems but rather the hymns, which often consist of two hundred lines (see Chapter IV). Indeed, some examplars of *Ludlul* (Tablet I text z, Tablet III text p, Tablet IV texts t and v) are divided by rulings into sections of ten lines as are the two-hundred-line hymns; these rulings do not, however, correspond to the structure of the poem but are purely mechanical and replace the number 10 (written with a wedge-head) often set at the margin of each tenth line in a variety of types of cuneiform texts, including other copies of Tablets I, II, and IV of *Ludlul*.[6]

Within this set number of lines the most common group is the distich, though distichs are not formally marked by either spacing or indentation. Their frequency is due to the device of parallelism as common in Babylonian poetry as it is in poetry written in other Semitic languages and in traditional oral poetry of a wide variety of peoples of the world.[7] Such parallelism consists in repeating a line or a pair of lines with only a minor change in the repeated version, or in pairing two lines built on syntactic parallelism and exhibiting either semantic parallelism or semantic opposition. However, the single tablets of this poem do not consist of sixty distichs, as a purely automatic distribution would presuppose; the distichs are interspersed with groups of three lines or more, and with single lines as well. The places where these single lines occur are, as we shall see, marked points in the flow of the poem.

The monologue character of the poem is established right at the outset: its first word, *ludlul* 'let me praise,' is a first-person optative form. The second element of the line, the noun phrase *bēl nēmeqi* 'lord of wisdom,' brings into play the divine savior. The god is named only in the second distich which, in accordance with the device of parallelism, is identical to the first except for adding the divine name Marduk to the phrase *bēl nēmeqi*. The divine savior does not intervene in the fate of the sufferer until Tablet III; nevertheless, his role is anticipated in the poem's first forty lines, and in fact in the very first line, since the sufferer's praise must needs go to the god who has saved him.[8]

The remainder of the first forty lines—18 distichs—then elaborate on the mercy of Marduk who, as often stated, may be wrathful but is also quick to relent. With line 41 the narrative sets in, introduced by "ever since my lord became angry with me and valiant Marduk turned from me in anger" and continuing with the description of the first set of misfortunes. The second tablet is of the same tenor; the sufferer enumerates the misfortunes that have befallen him even though he led a pious life and acted justly in carrying out his duties as a high official. The third tablet ushers in the deliverance, heralded by a set of three dreams, in which splendid figures appear in order to comfort the afflicted man. Indeed, his physical sufferings end, the contempt of his fellowmen is lifted from him, and thus in the fourth tablet he can describe his acts of thanksgiving to Marduk and the god's consort Ṣarpanitu, as he gives praise to the god and from his example also exhorts others to do likewise.

While the deliverance is not introduced until Tablet III, it is adumbrated earlier. Tablet I ends with the distich

> If only in the morning good (things) would come to me,
> . . . . the sun would dawn for me.

The mention of the sun—always written with the sign-group for Šamaš, the Sun god and the god of justice—assumes a special significance since the idioms "to see the sun," "to come out into the sunlight," and the like are the common metaphoric expressions for obtaining freedom, from misfortune as well as from prison. That the mention of the Sun god in the very last line of Tablet I is not without design is suggested by the fact that Tablet II also ends with the same word.[9] Tablet II, the second and last of the description of the suffering, and immediately followed by the hope-inspiring dream messages of Tablet III, uses the metaphor of the sun but not to allude to deliverance; on the contrary, on the threshold of the long-awaited deliverance the poet uses the image of the sun to express deepest despair, without even a ray of hope:

> The day has become dark for my entire family,
> For all my acquaintances their sun became covered over.

Since the end of Tablet III is not preserved and the end of Tablet IV is fragmentary, we cannot say whether the image of the sun closes these last two tablets or not. The image, significant in the first two when deliverance is yearned for, need not have appeared once the expectation had been fulfilled by Marduk; it is Marduk's name, not the Sun god's, that may have been given special prominence.

Of the poem's original length only about three-fourths (around 370 lines, many of them incomplete and fragmentary) has survived. The lack of attention to the compositional features of the poem is perhaps due to its fragmented state; Assyriologists may have also been put off by the seemingly unstructured and wordy descriptions of the sufferings, even in the best-preserved Tablet II. The poem's intricate texture becomes apparent upon a close reading. We will attempt such a reading on this completely preserved second tablet to illustrate the poetic structure of the text and incidentally the formal devices of such religious poems as prayers, penitential psalms, and hymns. These monologue-type genres share many devices as against—often dialogue-oriented—narrative poetry and what we may call incantatory poetry.

The distich arrangement of Tablet II begins only with line 4. The preceding three lines may be taken either as a three-line group or as a single line followed by a distich. Since lines 2 and 3 do not exhibit the parallelism or antithetical construction characteristic of distichs, the first three lines are best considered as one unit. Similar three-line groups also occur at lines 16-18, 36-38, 41-43, 68-70, 77-79?, and 99-101, while lines 48?, 90, and 116 seem to represent single-line units. Of the three-line groups some may be divided into distichs with a preceding or following single-line unit; thus lines 38, 43, 70, and 79 may be separated from the preceding two lines, and 99 from the following two. For example, if a typical distich is structured as, e.g., 97-98

> My arms are locked in the fetters of my flesh,
> My feet are *paralyzed* in the shackles of my own self,

then lines 100-101 also form the distich

> The whip that hit me is full of thorns,
> The goad that stung me is covered with barbs,

while line 99, "The blows given me are very painful, my wound is severe," is connected only semantically and not formally with the distich following it; this line, composed—just like the surrounding distichs—of two parts, but with the two parts divided between the two hemistichs, is then best considered a single-line unit. Similar cases may be made for the other apparent three-line units of this tablet.

Still, higher-level units may also be distinguished in this tablet; they do not constitute regular stanzas as they are of uneven length, nor are they marked on the written tablet by some external device such as a ruling. Yet they unmistakably form well-demarcated units, not merely by content or through the device of single lines interrupting a succession of distichs—this occurs only at line 70—but by the purely formal grammatical feature that each strophe begins with a verb form of the first person, a form beginning with the vowel *a*. It is this formal feature that first signals a new section. The signal is reinforced by the verb's marked position in line-initial; in Akkadian syntax the verb's unmarked position is at the end and not at the beginning of a clause, as we have pointed out in other contexts. The special function of these lines can be seen from the fact that no other line of this tablet begins with a comparable verb form; lines 5, 29, and 107 also have verbs at the head of the line, but in a form beginning with the vowel *u* which is characteristic not only of the first but of both the first and third persons. The *a*-initial verbs signal the beginning of strophe 1 at line 2, of strophe 2 at line 11, of strophe 3 at line 23, and of strophe 6 at line 95; strophe 5 (71-94) is introduced by the single-line unit of line 70. Strophe 4 alone has no such clear demarcation, although it seems probable that line 48 is a single-line unit, which then would signal the beginning of strophe 4 at line 49—too much of the text is missing in this strophe to be certain of its exact structure. The disjunction of strophes 2 and 3 is signaled, in addition, by the overlong line 22; while lines 21 and 22 run completely parallel, line 22 adds two words which have no parallel in the preceding line—an example rather of the figure called *concinnitas* than of strict parallelism.

The verses beginning with the first-person verb forms which introduce each strophe are also marked on the sound level. They contain a cumulation of sounds that contribute to the expressiveness, even though, as we shall see presently, they are not the only lines with expressive sound pattern. Strophe 2 is introduced by *āmur arkāte redāta ippiru* 'I looked behind me—persecution, catastrophe.' The dominating sound of the line is r which occurs four times; the next most frequent sounds are the dentals d and t which together occur three times. Since r was, most likely, alveolar, the line is characterized by seven apical (dental and alveolar) consonants.

The harshness of this line contrasts with the susurration in the introductory line of the next strophe (line 23): *ahsusma raman suppû teslītu* 'Yet I was mindful of prayer and supplication,' in which four sibilants appear beside the continuants h, m, n, r, l, as opposed to only three stops (one p and two t-s).

Strophe 3 is introduced at line 95 by *āhuz erši mēsiru mūṣê tāniḫu* 'I took to bed—a confinement; my leaving (the house) was *sighs*.' The three sibilants of this line—one voiced (z), one voiceless (s), one "emphatic" (ṣ)—are reinforced by the š in *erši*. The two m-s at the center—*mēsiru, mūṣê*—evoke murmur or moaning alongside the sibilants suggestive of sighs; this effect is enhanced by the great number of long vowels in this line.

Of the about thirty lines of this tablet that contain an unusual number of sound repetitions the single lines—those that are not paired with another in a distich—all exhibit this characteristic, for example, *ekâma ilmada alakti ili apâti* (38), *kî petê u katāmi ṭenšina šitni* (43), *mašâma namuššiša šepāja* (79). Phonologically most marked are three: line 48, *ana annâtu uštazzaq qerebšina la altanda* (4 n-s, three dentals); line 70, *kî uliltu annabik bubbāniš annadi* (as is shown by the spelling *bubbānis* instead of the normal *buppāniš* to emphasize the repetition of b-s), that is, the two lines which introduce strophes 4 and 5; and line 116, *kal mātija kî habil iqbûni,* which introduces the final section of the tablet. The most marked line of all, however, line 79, does not divide units; it is the last of a group of lines (73-79)—the three distichs 73-78—that are composed of three accent units as against the more common division into two hemistichs, and, like it, all contain a great number of m-s.

Each strophe may be further analyzed as to the pattern of its inner organization.

Strophe 2 (lines 11-22) after its introductory line is one long period, framed by "like one who" (line 12) and 'I became like" (line 22b), that is, "I became like one who. . . ." All eleven lines add either one or two elements of comparison. Being of an odd number, they can be considered as five distichs and a one-line verse, or as four distichs and one three-line verse, or as four distichs and three one-line verses. The first pattern appears in the first distich (12-13): each line contains one comparison:

> like one who established no libation to the god
> and did not remember the goddess with a food offering.

The next two lines—a distich or two single lines—introduce the second pattern: each of the two hemistichs of line 14 contains one comparison, while again, in line 15, only one comparison occurs:

> did not make obeisances, was unpracticed in bowing down,
> from whose mouth prayer and supplication ceased.

The next two distichs (16-17 and 19-20) have two comparisons in each line, that is, each hemistich contains one comparison. They are separated by line 18 which, like line 15, again contains one clause only. The last distich (21-22) is mixed as was the second distich, in that it contains two comparisons in the first line, and one in the second.

The alternation of the one-clause and two-clause lines is counterpointed by variations in the syntactic parallelism within each distich. This parallelism may be manifested by either a parallel or a chiastic sequence of corresponding elements. Parallel sequences—isocola—appear in lines 12-13: object—(indirect) object—predicate (12) and complement—object—predicate (13), as well as in the two hemistichs of line 14: object—predicate : object—predicate. In the distich made up of lines 16-17 the two clauses of the first line are parallel and those of the second line chiastic: predicate—object : predicate—object (16) *vs.* predicate—object : object—predicate (17). Line 18, with its single comparison, recalls line 15 and is in chiastic arrangement with it: complement—predicate—subject (15) *vs.* object—predicate—complement (18). The distich composed of lines 19-20 contains, first, a chiastic arrangement of the two hemistichs of each line and, second, a chiastic arrangement of the two lines with each other: object—predicate : predicate—object (19), predicate—object : object—predicate (20). In line 21 there are two isocola, each with the predicate at the end; line 22 that pairs with it has a single clause, but also has the predicate at the end.

Of the three lines with a single clause, 15, 18, and 22, two fill the hemistich which contains no predicate with two synonyms; in the first they function as the subject of the clause: *suppû teslītu* 'prayer (and) supplication' (15), and in the second as the object: *palāha it'udu* 'piety (and) respect' (18). The third defers the predicate, which in line 15 stands just before the caesura and in line 18 just after it, to the very end of the line: "Swore lightly the solemn oath by his god." The adverb *qalliš* 'lightly' that precedes the predicate *izkur* 'swore' is itself immediately preceded by the adjective *kabtu* 'solemn' which qualifies "oath"; since the literal meaning of *kabtu* is 'heavy,' the juxtaposition of these two words, "heavy" and "lightly," makes their contrast even greater and gives added weight to this, the last line of the strophe.

To sum up, in this strophe each line contains at least one verbal predicate, and some lines contain two, one in each hemistich. It is the placement of the predicate within the line and in relation to the predicates of the other lines that gives variety to the diction. That this variety is not an accident, nor required by the syntactic structure of the language, becomes apparent when we look at the third strophe, beginning with the first-person verb *ahsusma* 'I was mindful,' in line 23. The first three distichs of this strophe (23-28) contain not a single verb apart from the introductory "I was mindful." The distichs are completely parallel—isocola—as each consists of a nominal clause; the subject noun and the predicate noun are distributed across the two hemistichs in lines 25-28, and included in the same hemistich in line 24, which consists of two nominal clauses. This strophe, which extends most probably to line 48, contains, moreover, another distich (34-35) which also consists of nominal clauses. Only with the fourth distich (29-30) do clauses with verbal predicates begin to reappear. The verbs in the fourth and fifth distichs still refer to the actions of the hero of the story; the verb in the following single line (33) is an impersonal verb *(lu idi)* and serves as an exclamation. The next distich (34-35), again consisting of nominal clauses, then forms the transition to the remainder of the strophe; lines 36-47 have third-person subjects and contain general statements about mankind as a whole.

The fourth strophe begins either at line 48 or, should we consider this line with its first-person verb forms as the closing line to strophe 3, at line 49. Both of these lines begin with the preposition *ana* 'to,' perhaps not accidentally having an initial *a*-vowel, just like the verb-forms that introduced strophes 2 and 3. With line 48, whose predicate *altanda* 'I could (not) get at the heart (of the matter)' stands at the end of the line and not at the beginning, the first-person narrative returns. The return of the first person is reinforced in the next line (49) by the appearance of the first-person independent pronoun *jâti* in foreground position, *ana jâti šunuhu i . . . mehû* 'to me,' the weary one, a storm. . . ."

The next nine lines of the fourth strophe (50-58) turn to the enumeration of illnesses and demons which converge upon the sufferer; their impact on him is expressed solely by the grammatical device called "ventive," which provides a verb form with an ending that indicates the direction "hither." Only in the next eleven lines (59-69) is the specific impact on the sufferer detailed. He is affected in every part of his body; the enumeration begins, in the canonical order, with the head and continues with not only the limbs but also the inner organs, as if he ceased being a persona and existed only as dissected parts. The effect is summarized in line 70 which contains—though not in initial position—two first-person verbs:

> *kî ulilte annabik bubbāniš annadi* 'I fell flat like a *rush*, I was thrown face down'

and which marks, so it seems, the transition to a new strophe beginning with line 71.

Strophe 5 begins with the distich

> *alû zumrī ītediq ṣubāti* 'a demon put on my body for a garment'
> *kīma šuškalli ukattimanni šittu* 'like a net, sleep has swooped down upon me'

These are very strange similes indeed. The man's body is no longer his own: a demon has taken it over and dwells in it, as easily as if it were a mere outer garment, a covering under which the ego, the personality, is no longer itself but an alien, a demonic being. And while the second simile uses the familiar image of sleep swooping down and covering a person, here sleep not only covers but covers like a net, and specifically the net that soldiers use to capture enemies. It is not "sweet sleep" *(šittu ṭābtu)* gently descending, but a hostile, ensnaring, and benumbing sleep. As the following lines show, it is a sleep that is in fact one of those nightmares in which you are unable to move in order to escape from danger, a sleep that holds fast and paralyzes like the net thrown over the enemy or the hunted game.

This nightmare quality, this paralyzing effect is detailed with great precision in lines 73-79:

> My eyes are open but do not see;
> My ears are open but do not hear;
> Numbness has overcome my entire body,
> Paralysis has come upon my flesh,
> Stiffness has seized my arms,
> Debility has fallen on my loins,
> My feet have forgotten how to move.

The next few, fragmentary, lines continue the description but shift the emphasis slightly, it seems, from the dreamer's fright caused by the inability to move to its effect on the persons around him:

> They call to me, but I do not even answer
> those who inquire (82)
> My *family* weeps—I am not *conscious* (83)

The description of this demonic, nightmarish sleep, with its attendant horrors, effectively provides a foil for the dreams of Tablet III in which the dream apparitions are sent by the god to offer relief and which, therefore, presuppose the "sweet sleep" that has earlier eluded the sufferer.

With lines 84-94 the description of the sufferer's physical deterioration, while still using concrete imagery, is no longer in terms of a nightmare. His mouth is gagged, his throat constricted; food and drink are disgusting to him, and, perforce, for lack of nourishment he becomes emaciated, skin and bones (93).[10]

In the sixth strophe, beginning with *āhuz erši* 'I took to bed' (line 95), the self-presentation continues in a different mode. Parts of the body are no longer specified apart from such general terms as flesh, arms, feet, limbs:

> My arms are locked in the fetters of my flesh (97)
> My feet are *paralyzed* in the shackles of my own self (98)
> My limbs are splayed and lie awry (105).

The imagery is not that of paralysis of the body but that of prison, shackles, whip, scourge. The ultimate degradation is complete reduction to an animal existence:

> I spent the nights on my litter like an ox (106)
> I wallowed in my excrement like a sheep (107).

From this lowest point, comparable to animal existence only, we suddenly return to civilization, with the aid of a device which integrates the long and seemingly diffuse complaint into the overall structure of Tablet II. The seventh and final strophe (108-120) of Tablet II takes us back to the beginning by repeating the first strophe, but in a mirror fashion. The repetition is not verbatim, but the key words at least of the first strophe recur in the final one. These key terms refer to the practitioners who, according to the accepted socio-religious order of things, can provide relief and redress through their expertise in sounding out the divine will and performing the appropriate rites for reconciling man with his god. They are the diviners—the haruspex and the dream-interpreter—who can find out what the future holds in store; the diagnostician who can foretell the outcome of the disease; and the exorcist who can propitiate the angry god by appropriate rituals. The recurrence of these motifs can be seen from the juxtaposition of these two strophes:

Strophe 1
    1. This year and into the next the expected time (of deliverance)
         went by.
      I look around: Evil, nothing but evil.
      My hardship has increased, I find no good fortune.
      I called to the *god* but he did not turn his face to me,
    5. I prayed to the *goddess,* but she did not lift her head to me.

> The *haruspex* could not give a verdict through extispicy,
> Through libanomancy the dream-interpreter could not clear up my case.
> I invoked the god of dreams but he gave me no insight,
> The *exorcist* with his rites did not dispel the divine wrath.
> 10. What strange goings-on everywhere!

Strophe 7
> 108. The *exorcist* shied away from my symptoms
> And the *haruspex* confused my omens.
> 110. The diagnostician could not clear up the nature of my illness
> And the *haruspex* could not set a term for my sickness.
> The *god* did not come to help me, did not take my hand,
> The *goddess* did not take pity on me, did not go at my side.
> Open is the grave, my funerary offerings are prepared,
> 115. Before my being dead the wake was over.

Lines 4 and 5, with their reference to *ilu* 'god' and *ištaru* 'goddess' are resumed by lines 112-113; 6, with its reference to *bārû* 'haruspex', by 111; and 9, with its reference to *mašmašu* 'exorcist' by 108. There is no exact correspondent to the dream-interpreter (7), or the god of dreams (8); they are replaced by *āšipu* 'diagnostician' (110) and by the repetition of *bārû* 'haruspex', in lines 109 and 111. The failure of the gods to respond to the sufferer's plight is expressed by reference to "his (the god's) face," "her (the goddess's) head" in lines 4 and 5; lines 112 and 113, which echo them even as far as the mention of parts of the body, now speak of the sufferer: "my hand," "my side." Line 115, "Before my being dead the wake was over," may even contain a subtle reference to the first verse of the tablet, *šattamma ana balāṭ* 'This year and into the next,' since *balāṭ* 'next year' is the same word as *balāṭ* 'life' to which would correspond, by opposition, *mītūti* 'my being dead' of line 115.

To the first three lines containing the general statement about the man's suffering correspond the last seven of the tablet. "Evil" and "hardship" now take the concrete form of the grave readied and the mourning in progress: "All my land said: 'What a pity!' " All the while the man's ill-wishers gloat. This gloating is described by verbs denoting brightness:

> My ill-wisher heard it and his face shone, (117)
> They gave the news to the woman ill-wisher and her mood brightened, (118)

in a distich which contrasts the more with the last distich with its words for darkness and gloom:

> The day has become dark for my entire family, (119)
> For all my acquaintances their sun became covered over. (120)

It is from this unrelieved gloom into which the sufferer has been plunged that he will be delivered by his god. The second half of the poem depicts the ascent from deepest despair and the physical and emotional recovery from utter misery. Yet the next tablet begins with an outcry *de profundis*: *kabtat qāssu ul ale'i našâša* 'His hand is heavy, I cannot bear it!'—a line whose placement at the head of Tablet III has been a bit puzzling: a reference to the clemency of the god would surely have been more in place here. It is thanks to one of the happy though rare accidents in Assyriology that we can now place this line in its proper perspective. I have alluded to the recent recovery of the first part of the poem (note 8). There, among the traits of Marduk enumerated in lines 1-36, we find the line (33): *ana kî kabtat qāssu libbašu rēmēni* 'his heart is merciful toward him (who says) "How heavy his hand is!"' Thus the first line of Tablet III effectively signals that, while still *in profundis*, we have turned the tide: he whose hand is heavy is also the one who is merciful. We are indeed on the road of ascent that is gradually described in this tablet. In the final tablet the redeemed hero enters Babylon to give thanks and praise to Marduk in a *magnificat* promised, as we now see in the newly recovered introduction, in lines 37-40 of the first tablet. As he passes through the gates of the temple Esagil, he receives at each gate the grace that is embodied in it through its name. The poet, as we remarked earlier, is also a scholar, displaying his scholarship by interpreting the Sumerian names of the gates. But he is no mere scholarly commentator; he does not simply translate these names into Akkadian as we often find in the numerous extant lists of temples, gates, and even of the streets of Babylon,[11] but finds for each name an application to the progressive restoration of the hero's state of grace and to his acts of thanksgiving.

ina Ká.hé.gál hegalla inna[dnanni]	At the Gate of Abundance abundance was bestowed on me;
ina Ká.^dLamma.ra.bi lamassī iṭṭeh[anni]	At the Gate of the Protective Spirit, my protective spirit approached me;
ina Ká.silim.ma šulmāna appalis	At the Gate of Welfare I set eyes on *welfare*;
ina Ká.nam.ti.la balāṭu ammahir	At the Gate of Life, I was received into life;

ina Ká.^dUtu.UD.è itti baltūti ammani	At the Gate of Sunrise, I was reckoned among the living;
ina Ká.u₆.di.babbar.ra iddātūa immera	At the Gate of Clear Signs my signs became clear;
ina Ká.nam.tag.ga.du₈.a i'ilti ippaṭir	At the Gate of Absolving Sins my sin was absolved;
ina Ká.ka.tar.ra ištāla pija	At the Gate of Inquisition they interrogated me;
ina Ká.a.še.er.du₈.ù.da uptaṭṭara tānīhī	At the Gate of Dissolving Sighs my sighs were dissolved;
ina Ká.a.sikil.la mê tēlilte assalih	At the Gate of Holy Water I was sprinkled with water of purification;
ina Ká.silim.ma itti Marduk annamir	At the Gate of Reconciliation I met Marduk;
ina Ká.hi.li.sù \<ana\> šēp Ṣarpanītu annabik	At the Gate of Charm I fell at the feet of Ṣarpanītu.[12]

This enumeration which takes us to line 50 of Tablet IV is also the last connected section of the poem. The remaining disconnected pieces of this tablet have been variously fitted together;[13] they recount the sacrifices offered in gratitude and exhort the entire world to praise Marduk. The very last lines are fragmentary and have thus far defied attempts at reconstructing the conclusion of this learned poem—another sign of its unconventional character.

Ludlul bēl nēmeqi
Tablet II

Translation

This year and into the next, the expected time (of deliverance) went by.
I look around: Evil, nothing but evil.
My hardship has increased, I find no good fortune.
I called to the god, but he did not turn his face to me,
5   I prayed to the goddess, but she did not lift her head to me.
The haruspex could not give a verdict through extispicy,
Through libanomancy the dream-interpreter could not clear up my case.
I invoked the god of dreams but he gave me no insight,
The exorcist with his rites did not dispel the divine wrath.
10 What strange goings-on everywhere!

I looked behind me—persecution, catastrophe.
Like one who established no libation to the god
And did not remember the goddess with a food offering,
Did not make obeisances, was unpracticed in bowing down,
15 From whose mouth prayer and supplication ceased,
Who stopped celebrating feasts, disdained the holy day,
Became neglectful, despised their (the gods') ordinances,
Did not instruct his household in piety and respect for the gods,
Did not invoke his god, ate the food meant for him,
20 Abandoned his goddess, brought her no burnt flour offering,
Like one who *aggrandized himself*, forgot his lord,
Swore lightly the solemn oath by his god, I became like.

Yet I was mindful of prayer and supplication,
Prayer was my conscious way of life, sacrifice my rule.
25 The day of worshipping the god was my pleasure,
The day of following the goddess profit and gain.
Homage to the king was my joy,
And making music for him was indeed a pleasure for me.
I instructed my land in the observance of the gods' decrees,
30 I taught my people to honor the name of the goddess.
I made the songs of praise to the king like unto those to a god,
And taught the population respect for the palace.
If only I knew that these things are pleasing to the god!
What seems good to oneself is a sin to one's god.
35 What is distasteful to one's feelings is good to one's god.
Who can understand the will of the gods in heaven?
Who can comprehend the decisions of those of the abyss?

Where have human beings understood the way of the god?
He who was alive yesterday died today,
40 One moment he was dejected, in the next he becomes boisterous.
One instant he sings a joyous song,
In a trice he moans like a professional wailer.
Men's mood changes like day to night.
When they are hungry, they become like corpses,
45 When they are sated, they vie with their god.
In good circumstances they talk about ascending to heaven,
But when they grow depressed they speak of going down to the nether world.
I have been considering these things but could not get at the heart of the matter.

To me, the weary one, a storm has . . . .
50 An illness sapping my strength has pounced upon me,
The evil wind has risen against me from the horizon,
From the very bowels of the earth the head ailment grew towering over me.
An evil spirit came out of the depths, its abode,
An indeflectible ghost came at me from the nether world,
55 The Lamaštu demon came down from the mountain fastness,
Cold shivers *receded* with the high water,
Decay cleaves the ground along with the grass.
Banding together, their entire cohort attacked me.
They struck me on the head, enveloped my skull,
60 They made my face somber, my eyes brim with tears,
They bent my neck, made my neck muscles go limp,
They hit me in the chest, they tore out my nipples,
Invaded my flesh, afflicted it with spasms,
Lit a fire in my stomach,
65 Churned my bowels, twisted my entrails,
. . . . , affected my chest,
Affected even my limbs, and made my *diaphragm* quake,
My tall body they wrecked like a wall,
My robust figure they bent over like a bulrush.
70 I fell flat like a *rush*, I was thrown face down.

A demon put on my body for a garment;
Like a net, sleep has swooped down upon me.
My eyes are open but do not see;
My ears are open but do not hear;
75 Numbness has overcome my entire body,
Paralysis has come upon my flesh,
Stiffness has seized my arms,
Debility has fallen on my loins,

My feet have forgotten how to move.
80 My firm [. . .] *collapsed suddenly,*
The . . . of death has covered my face.
They call to me, but I do not even answer those who inquire,
My *family* weeps—I am not *conscious.*
A snare is laid in my mouth,
85 And a bolt is a bar for my lips.
My gate is barred, my drinking place blocked
. . . is my hunger, constricted my throat.
I swallow the fine cereal—it tastes like strinkweed,
Even beer, the sustenance of the people, has become distasteful to me.
90 Verily, the disease has become protracted.
For lack of food my countenance has altered for the worse,
My flesh has wasted away, my blood has ebbed,
My bones are visible, covered only by skin,
My veins are distended, *they are struck by jaundice.*

95 I took to bed—a confinement; my leaving (the house) was *sighs.*
My house has turned into a prison for me.
My arms are locked in the fetters of my flesh,
My feet are *paralyzed* in the shackles of my own self.
The blows given me are very painful, my wound is severe.
100 The whip that hit me is full of thorns,
The goad that stung me is covered with barbs.
All day long a persecutor pursues me,
At night he does not let me respire for an instant.
My sinews are parted through displacement,
105 My limbs are splayed and lie awry.
I spent the nights on my litter like an ox,
I wallowed in my excrement like a sheep.
The exorcist shied away from my symptoms,
And the haruspex confused my omens.
110 The diagnostician could not clear up the nature of my illness
And the haruspex could not set a term for my sickness.
The god did not come to help me, did not take my hand,
The goddess did not take pity on me, did not go at my side.
Open is the grave, my funerary offerings are prepared,
115 Before my being dead the wake was over.
All my land said: "What a pity!"
My ill-wisher heard it and his face shone,
They gave the news to the woman ill-wisher and her mood brightened.
The day has become dark for my entire family,
For all my acquaintances their sun became covered over.

NOTES

1. A. Leo Oppenheim, The Interpretation of Dreams in the Ancient Near East, 1956, p. 216.

2. An exception is the article by W. von Soden, "Das Fragen nach der Gerechtigkeit Gottes im Alten Orient," MDOG 96 (1965) 41-59.

3. For instance, the myth of Anzû (see Chapter III). For a discussion of the introductory patterns of narrative poetry see C. Wilcke, "Die Anfänge der akkadischen Epen," ZA 67 (1977) 153-216.

4. *Šurpu*. A Collection of Sumerian and Akkadian Incantations, edited by E. Reiner (= Archiv für Orientforschung, Beiheft 11), Graz, 1958; Die assyrische Beschwörungssammlung *Maqlû*, edited by Gerhard Meier (= Archiv für Orientforschung, Beiheft 2), Berlin, 1937.

5. As, for example, the division of the *Divina Commedia* into three times 33 cantos.

6. The equivalence of rulings and 10-signs has also been noted by M. Vogelzang, RA 73 (1979) 180.

7. See Roman Jakobson, "Grammatical Parallelism and Its Russian Facet," Language 42 (1966) 399-429. For further literature see James J. Fox, "Roman Jakobson and the Comparative Study of Parallelism," in *Roman Jakobson: Echoes of His Scholarship*. Daniel Armstrong and C. H. van Schooneveld, eds. Lisse: The Peter de Ridder Press, 1977, pp. 59-90.

8. These first forty lines, until recently only incompletely known, are now available on a duplicate published by D. J. Wiseman, Anatolian Studies 30 (1980), 101-107.

9. Also noted by J. S. Cooper, JCS 27 (1975) 249 and note 9. This, of course, brings to mind the *Divina Commedia*, where all three parts end with the word *stelle*, "stars."

10. See Edith Porada, "An Emaciated Male Figure of Bronze in the Cincinnati Art Museum," *Studies Presented to A. Leo Oppenheim* (Chicago: 1964) 159-166.

11. See O. R. Gurney, "The Fifth Tablet of 'The Topography of Babylon,' " Iraq 36 (1974) 39-52.

12. Tablet IV, lines 39-50 (numbered in Lambert's edition 79-90). The Akkadian interpretations of the Sumerian names of the gates are not always equivalent to a literal translation of their component elements; in such cases, the English translation follows the poet's interpretation describing the pilgrim's experience at that gate. Thus, the name of the sixth gate is, in reality, "Gate of Brilliant Admiration," but the word u_6.di "admiration" or "wonderment" seems to have been taken as the similarly written *gizkim* "sign, portent," to which corresponds the Akkadian *id(d)ātūa* "my signs"; the name of the eighth gate contains the word *ka.tar* "praise, lauds" but was interpreted as *ka* = *pû* "mouth" and *(èn).tar* = *šâlu* "to

interrogate." The name of the third gate contains the word *silim* which otherwise is equivalent to *šulmu* "well-being" or *salīmu* "reconciliation" not, as here, to *šulmānu* "present"; when this name recurs as the name of the eleventh gate, the interpretation, just as for gates five and twelve, is not obviously connected with the components of the name. The experience related to the twelfth gate (line 50) is subject to two analyses: we may read either, inserting *ana*, <*ana*> *šēp Ṣarpanitu annabik* or *šēp Ṣarpanītu annašiq* "I kissed the feet of Ṣarpanitu," assuming an unusual stem form for the verb "to kiss"; this is an attractive alternative as we now see that verb forms of the passive or ingressive "fourth" or N-stem abound in these lines (39, 41, 45, 48, 49), even when they are incorrect as in *ammahir* (line 42) or only appear to be such forms (line 40).

13. The poem ends with the lines that in Lambert's edition are numbered 1-15, 24-50, see von Soden, MDOG 94 (1975) 51 n. 5. For a somewhat different suggestion for the ordering of the fragments of Tablet IV, see M. Vogelzang, RA 73 (1979) 180.

RETROSPECT AND PROSPECT

At this point, the reader might expect a conclusion, an overview of the lessons learned from this sampler of Babylonian poetry. On the contrary. The selections, intended as case studies to illustrate the variety of range (historical, mythological, lyric) of this poetry and of the approaches that can serve to integrate it into the *fundus* of Western literature, for this very reason present each text in its uniqueness and not as representative of a tradition or genre, as a different emphasis, say, on the scope and richness of this literature, might have done. Only rarely could similarities between a particular poetic work and others exhibiting the same motifs and treatment be pointed out; such connections—in essence, what contemporary literary criticism likes to term "intertextuality"—are meaningful only for the reader familiar with the entire poetic corpus, and then often only in the original language. They require "literary competence," defined as "the reader's familiarity with the descriptive systems, with themes, with his society's mythologies, and above all with other texts" (M. Riffaterre, *Semiotics of Poetry* [Indiana University Press 1978] p. 5). Anticipatory and retardatory devices, part of the poetic technique, need to be exemplified on longer texts, whether epic or prose. Of the poetic fabric—the sound patterns, the rhythm—only a few examples could be shown since these elements are best perceived in the original language. However few, these examples testify to the fact that sound effects, and even sound symbolism, were not neglected in a poetry whose main poetic devices are syntactic.

Nor is our knowledge of Babylonian poetry exhausted. The chances of discovery bring to light, as we witness all the time, completely novel poems and genres along with copies of well-known texts. About thirty years ago a complete copy of a unique humorous poem was recovered, a poem whose folktale parallels are evident, as shown by O. R. Gurney in *Anatolian Studies* 22 (1972) 149-158; just recently another humorous poem, although in a different vein, was published, reminding us that what seems unique and atypical may simply reflect an accident of discovery. At some future time not only will these humorous poems need to be studied as a literary form but our perception of Babylonian literature as solemn, religious, and serious will have to be reconsidered as well.

Equally important, some of the features that here emerged from the analysis of a particular poem may play a different role in another. The differences, that must reflect both historical time depth and different poetic traditions, can rarely be recaptured: the anonymity of the Babylonian poet is breached but rarely and even then sanctioned only by such devices as the author's name revealed in an acrostic. Dialogue, that in a narrative poem provides variety and in a philosophical one is a device for expressing introspection, can be so prevalent in some poems as to suggest dramatic performance. Repetition, that in a folk-song-type ditty is simple diction, is the mark of artifice amid the learned vocabulary of "wisdom" literature or of the royal narratives. Creation can be described in an epic manner as the aftermath of a theomachia in the "Poem of Creation" or in a few concatenated lines of a charm, and history in terms of the king's divinely ordained exploits in the royal annals or as the inevitable transfer of rule from dynasty to dynasty—*regnum a gente in gentem transfertur*—in chronicles and prophecies; the different expressions that these topics take on also shape their content.

Babylonian literature speaks with many voices. So too, many interpreters are needed to bring it into the purview of the non-specialist, be it through translation or through a close reading, for which the expert alone is qualified. I would hope that some of my fellow Assyriologists, philologists in the widest sense, who love the ancient text not as a repository of strange and obscure words and grammatical forms but as the product of a culture that can be understood and enjoyed, will engage not only in providing text editions destined for the scholars in the field but also in opening up to others the poetic works of ancient Babylonia.